Seeing through Symbols

INSIGHTS INTO SPIRIT

Edited by Carol S. Lawson & Robert F. Lawson

In Six Parts Introduced by Robert H. Kirven

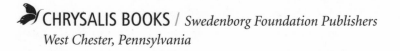
CHRYSALIS BOOKS / *Swedenborg Foundation Publishers*
West Chester, Pennsylvania

THE CHRYSALIS READER is a book series that examines themes related to the universal quest for wisdom. Inspired by the Swedenborg Foundation journal *Chrysalis,* each volume presents original short stories, essays, poetry, and art exploring the spiritual dimensions of a chosen theme. Works are selected by the series editors. For information on future themes or submission of original writings, contact Carol S. Lawson, Route 1, Box 184, Dillwyn, Virginia 23936.

© 1998 by the Swedenborg Foundation

Printed on recycled paper and bound in the United States of America

LIBRARY OF CONGRESS CATALOGING-IN-PUBLICATION DATA
Seeing through symbols: insights into spirit / edited by Carol S. Lawson
& Robert F. Lawson
    p.   cm. — (Chrysalis Reader; v. 5)
  ISBN 0-87785-229-4 (pbk.)
  1.Spiritual life—Literary collections. 2. American literature—20th century
3. Symbolism—Literary collections.
I. Lawson, Carol S. II. Lawson, Robert F., 1948– . III. Series
PS509.S62S44 1998   98-28707
810.8′038—dc21   CIP

CHRYSALIS BOOKS
Swedenborg Foundation Publishers
320 North Church Street
West Chester, Pennsylvania 19380

Contents

EDITOR'S NOTE
Robert F. Lawson vii

FOREWORD
Existence as Symbolic viii
Wilson Van Dusen

PART I: THE THIRD EYE: FRAMES FOR SEEING
Transitions / Charms (poems) 2, 3
Rebecca Lee Yates / Ginnie Goulet Gavrin

Wyeth's Windows (essay) 4
T. M. Moore

St. Teresa and the Seven Chakras (essay) 9
Linda Holt

Homebody (essay) 18
Perry S. Martin

Where the Answers Are (story) 24
Anne McGinley

Neighborhood Watch (story) 30
Steven Cartwright

PART II: INTERLOCKING STITCHES: MEMENTOS WE HOLD
Interlocking Stitches / Contemplating the Shroud (poems) . . . 38, 39
Tonia Triebwasser / Fredrick Zydek

Pretend Friends (story) 41
Ruth Latta

Cassandra in the Temple (essay) 49
Betty Bone Schiess

A Houseful of Guests (essay) 52
Kathryn Jane Ripley

The House That George Haunts (story) 57
W. Joe Innis

Lawn Doctor (story) 61
Michael Robartes

Chinese Wedding (story) 64
Paul and Eng-li Green

PART III: ROSES UNFOLDING: COMPLETE IN THE MOMENT
Nautilus / Flowers for Dad's Birthday (poems) 70, 71
Arlene Distler / Duane Tucker

Tintern Abbey (story) 72
Jan Shoemaker

The Prodigals (story) 76
Sylvia Shaw

The Way of Flowers (essay) 85
    Joan D. Stamm

Beyond the Blue (story) 91
    Susan Picard

PART IV: THE OTHER SIDE OF THE LOOKING GLASS

Gila River Sycamores / Invention of the Paper Clip (poems) . . 96, 97
    Suzanne Freeman / I. E. Steele

The Icon of Sophia (essay) 98
    Walter R. Christie

Outside Mombasa (essay) 107
    J. T. Hullett

Rituals Stay, Symbols Follow (essay) 115
    Adam Seward

Mirrors of Meaning (essay) 119
    John L. Hitchcock

PART V: YESTERDAY'S TRACKS

The Egg Shell / The Tin Man's Goodbye (poems) 128, 129
    Carol Lem / P. J. Ruschmann

Yesterday's Tracks (story) 131
    R. H. Herzog

Family Tree (story) 133
    Patte LeVan

Claims (story) 141
    Vincent DeCarolis

Sun Tzu and the Art of Spiritual Warfare 146
    Grant R. Schnarrr

Some Kind of Sign (story) 152
    Lani Wright

PART VI: FOLLOW THE PLEIADES

Inis Meáin / Inishmaan (poems) 156, 157
    Paul Finn

The Dance (story) 158
    Jan Frazier

Symbols among the Angels (story) 162
    Donald L. Rose

In Praise of Trees (story) 165
    Catherine Lazers Bauer

Jimmy Christ (essay) 169
    John L. Hitchcock

Flying (story) 173
    Don Kissil

Symbols

THE OTHER NIGHT I DREAMED I was sleeping in the mountains. The postman put stamps on my ears. The image of a person being mailed could be a modern-day equivalent of Aladdin's magic carpet to any-where. Of course, that's just one interpretation. And that's the mys-tery of symbols—transportable touchstones that can transform in the twinkling of an eye. Another dream: A man wearing a cowboy hat stands in the desert holding a dusty rock. He says this is a God-for-saken land. On closer examination, however, the rock is quartz, and its crystals flash red and green like sheet lightning. Is this a promise of rain?

The scientist and mystic Emanuel Swedenborg, eponym of the Swedenborg Foundation, publisher of Chrysalis Books, began his spiritual journey by keeping a dream journal. Later, he devoted much of his theological writing to a detailed system that could be titled, "Seeing through Symbols." His favorite term for insights into spirit was "correspondences," and he saw the whole physical universe as an infinitely complex representation of spiritual reality.

Sometimes I wonder if the act of painting is not at its core the same process perfected by mystics—dreamers half-awake, who are neither in nor out of focus but in a practiced state of soft focus. Joe Innis, whose painting illustrates one of the stories in this book, says, "Don't ask an artist what his paintings mean. If he's any good at what he does, he probably can't tell you."

Some writers, especially poets, have reported that it is while in a state of semi-wakefulness that symbolic language comes to the mind's surface and lends its power to the formation of realities at hand. Could it be that the work of art that makes sense to the be-holder, whether it be music in a concert hall or a stone carving in a cathedral, has reached into the very center of the beholder? If there is resonance between artist and viewer, perhaps it is because anoth-er language exists in all of us. Swedenborg saw angels bypass words and "read" the content of their companions' faces. That is a shared reality of dreamers, and that is the looking-glass for seeing through symbols.

Existence as Symbolic

Lee Lawrie, sculptor.
The Owl of Wisdom
Bronze doorknob (detail)
on foyer entrance
to library, ca. 1924.
National Academy
of Sciences,
Washington, D.C.
Shonna Valeska,
photographer, 1984,
New York.

SYMBOLS ARE A MEANS OF REPRESENTING WHAT IS HIGHER by means of something lower and simpler. Signs, in contrast, are arbitrarily chosen for meaning. "Don't Enter" is a sign. But a hand, drawn as though to halt anyone, is a symbol.

The meaning of symbols is suggested in their form, but understanding and appreciation are needed for a symbol to become living and meaningful. When there was widespread illiteracy, symbols were prevalent and powerful because they represented how people felt without the use of written language. Over time, without the verbal descriptions of their meanings, a culture's common symbols can be lost and only partly recovered with much effort, as in the pictorial language of the Mayans. When the meaning of a symbol is lost, it becomes an empty sign. For it to come back to life, someone needs to understand and appreciate all it represents. Symbols do not have power in themselves but only through human minds that perceive them. To be alive, a symbol must resonate with meaning in a person.

The early persecuted Christians relied on symbols they could easily draw, whose meanings were known to the in-group.[1] "Jesus Christ, God's Son, Savior" spelled *fish* in Greek, which was drawn in a simple outline. The fish could live only in water just as Christians lived only in the water of baptism. Also St. Peter was a fisherman, trained to be a fisher of men. A symbol can have many layers of meaning.

Often a symbol's meaning was based on the legend associated with it. The crane came to represent good order in the monastic life. The bird stands tall and majestically, moves with dignity, and represents loyalty, good life, and good works. The legend was that cranes at night gather in a circle around their king, just as monks do in religious services. Cranes often sleep with one foot tucked up, but legend had it that the guardian crane kept a stone in the foot that, when dropped, woke the others.

Symbols come alive if their symbolism is explained. Because the Jews used to sacrifice oxen, for example, the ox came to represent the Jewish nation itself. Oxen show much patience and strength while laboring for the good of others. Similarly the Jewish nation labored patiently and long (in Christian symbolism) as a precursor to Christianity. A symbol is born when it is seen to represent something higher. And, if we meditate on a symbol, more meanings emerge. *The symbol is condensed meaning.*

Oddly enough we each retain a symbol-making capacity in our sleep. We awaken in our inner world to meet and deal with our own symbols. Some special dreams may have several layers of meanings. Isn't it strange that we have this natural capacity for symbols that shows up every night whether we care or not?

On one level, the symbol exists as a limited item that signifies something that can be internally appreciated. But the great spiritual adventurers turn this process around in the belief that all things we see and experience, even ourselves, are essentially symbols of something higher. They found the whole of creation and every part of it symbolic. In the Hindu *Upanishads,* some of the oldest religious literature in existence, only Brahman, the incomprehensible Ultimate

One, exists. All levels of existence symbolize this One, and the universe is like a giant stupa that widens in coming down from its top to its base in the material world. This idea transforms the symbol from a little image we can examine into an example of the Creator's work. Another spiritual explorer, Emanuel Swedenborg (1688–1772), had a similar insight.

Swedenborg believed that the Life of the Lord creates downward through corresponding heavens, through the interior of the person an and through the person's body and all of material creation. The whole of creation is a theater of successive levels of manifestation.

> Everything that appears in the universe in any way is a representation of God's governing, to such an extent that there is nothing at all in the universe—in the starry sky above, or on this planet and its three kingdoms below—which is not in its own way representative. Indeed, each and every thing in the natural order is an ultimate image: the Divine issues forth into celestial creations and actions, which are expressions of what is good; from these come spiritual things expressing what is true; and out of the former and the latter natural things appear.[2]

This process is easiest to see by looking at ourselves. When we express what we feel, our invisible inner spiritual life affects our visible facial expressions, gestures, words, and movements. When what is internal expresses itself faithfully, these outer material features are congruent with our inner spirit. This is the lower level of a process that begins with God creating through the heavens and through our inner life to manifest in our outer form. Our self-expression is a direct working of this universal process.[3]

But what if we try to feign our inner feeling, pretending one thing when we feel another? Because the outer does not so well match the inner, Swedenborg uses the term 'representation' for this. A representation is a partial but not as faithful an image of the inner spiritual. If you look closely when feigning, you will see the tension of the effort to show one thing while feeling another. The inner life is still showing, but two contrary trends are showing. The lie detector test measures the underlying physiology of this tension of opposites. But when people are harmoniously expressing what is in them, what shows outwardly corresponds to their inner lives. This process is automatic; it is simply how we live. It requires more effort to pretend.

In Hinduism, all below the level of Brahman are *maya*, illusion. Because only the ultimate One really exists, all the rest is illusion. Similarly, Swedenborg concludes that only God really exists, but he sees a use in knowing how these levels of creation correspond to the One. For Swedenborg, this universal process creates and sustains itself.

How might the human eye, for example, correspond to the spiritual world? For the moment we want to treat it as a symbol of something higher. Do we take apart the eye to try to grasp its spiritual aspect? No. What it represents spiritually is shown by the use it serves for us. The eye sees. It corresponds spiritually to perception and understanding. Through looking at the uses of things we can move directly into their spiritual implications. As an ancient symbol, one eye alone represented the all-seeing eye of God or God's wisdom. In the Vedic tradition, for example, the third eye represents another way of seeing.

But what of ego or self-identity? Swedenborg says it is given to us, a gift of love which makes us feel real and in control. Our egos allow us to experience higher conscience, to feel responsible to ourselves and to others. Yet, even self-identity, something given to us out of God's love, is not substantial in itself. It also arises out of this universal process by which the higher represents itself at ever lower or outer levels.

Swedenborg makes clear that this process of creating correspondences and representations is like a ladder given to us. We can climb up this ladder back to the Source.[4] What does it take to climb back up the ladder? To identify with the material body as our real self anchors us to a lower level. If we identify with ego, we are at a higher level but still identified with merely a stage in the whole process. To begin the ascent up the ladder, we need to recognize and respect the universal process by which the higher clothes itself with the lower. Our inner life and our attempt to discover and express what is in us is a near-at-hand example of the climb up the ladder.[5]

There are a number of corollaries in the practice of acknowledging and respecting this universal process. We are not in it, but rather we exist outside it. Hell or evil are separate from this universal process and opposed to it. Respecting this life given us, we respect all other forms of creation. To truly see and respect this universal process in no way limits our powers. Rather we come to understand

Paddy Jupurrurla Nelson, Paddy Japaljarri Sims, Larry Jungarrayi Spencer. *Yanjilypiri Jukurrpa (Star Dreaming)*. Synthetic polymer paint on canvas, 372 × 171.4 cm., 1985. National Gallery of Australia, Canberra.

that our feeble powers are given to us. We become a bit more modest regarding ourselves.

Swedenborg's description of this universal principle of creation by correspondences is vast and challenging to contemplate. He wrote a long section on the subject in his *Heaven and Hell* because this unitary principle runs through his experiences in spiritual worlds beyond this one.[6] The concept knits together the whole of creation in a single, simple design.

The thought that in the end only God exists accords with my own spiritual discoveries. I respect the ancient Hindu *Upanishads,* for these ancient explorers found this to be true as well. I can understand why the Hindus, based on this truth, dismiss all the rest of creation as an illusion. In a sense they are correct. Yet I see great use in Swedenborg's hammering out the implications at all the lesser levels including our own. All else may be ultimately an illusion, but isn't it a very great and substantial one, one worth understanding?

So how did we get from a simple symbol to the universal principle which makes all of creation a theater of levels of symbols? A symbol is not simply a device to represent what is higher by the lower, as Christianity by a cross, Islam by a crescent, and Buddhism by the wheel of life. We have an innate capacity for symbols even in our sleep. Why? Because our very lives are part of a universal process by which what is higher takes on lower representations of itself. It is part of our nature, how we live, and how all else exists. When we discover and honor this process, we are in harmony with all aspects of our nature. We are living symbols in the midst of a universe of living symbols, with portents everywhere.

Notes

1. George Ferguson. *Signs and Symbols in Christian Art.* Oxford University Press, New York, 1961.

2. Emanuel Swedenborg. *Arcana Coelestia.* Paragraph 3483. Swedenborg Foundation, West Chester, Pennsylvania. Swedenborg numbered the paragraphs in his works. In Swedenborgian studies it is customary to reference a particular text by the book's title and Swedenborg's paragraph number, as those numbers are uniform in all editions.

3. *Ibid.* Paragraph 3628.

4. *Ibid.* Paragraph 4323.

5. Wilson Van Dusen. *Returning to the Source.* Swedenborg Foundation, West Chester, Pennsylvania, 1997.

6. Emanuel Swedenborg. *Heaven and Hell.* Paragraphs 87–115. Swedenborg Foundation, West Chester, Pennsylvania, various editions.

Seeing through Symbols

INSIGHTS INTO SPIRIT

PART I

The Third Eye
Frames for Seeing

SEEING THROUGH SYMBOLS
is something like looking through a window.
If we look *at* a window, we see glass;
but if we look *through* it,
we see something outside our present frame of reference.
When psychologists speak of a "third eye"
through which we see
a dimension hidden from the first two,
they refer to an expanded vision
that comes from this special kind of seeing.

A curtain moved by a sea breeze is a symbol,
as are the concentric defenses of a castle,
or the ascending series of chakras
in the philosophy of yoga,
or a wolf in the forest.
Your body is a symbol—or may become one,
since it often represents
very different meanings to others who see it
than it does to you who are living in it.
Violent acts are symbols,
as are acts of love.

—ROBERT H. KIRVEN

REBECCA LEE YATES

Transitions

The water being low in Oneonta Gorge
with no rain for weeks,
we found small rocks to take us
across the creek
and back again
to reach a place where we met the cliff face with our hands.
Like reading braille our fingers moved,
feeling all the stories that water has told to stone,
messages from everywhere.

We stopped at the point where walls curled away
to where we couldn't see.
Deep water stood so still there,
so still and clear we knelt.
It held our breath.

That's the place where my world begins,
before decisions, before change,
where everything depends
on all you can and cannot see.

Above deep water I take a breath
and stand at those curves and ask. . . .
Tell me? What is written in stone?

REBECCA LEE YATES has a law degree from Northwestern School of Law, Lewis and Clark College, in Portland, Oregon, and a degree in geography from Louisiana State University, in Baton Rouge. Her poetry has appeared in *The American Scholar, Daughters of Sarah,* and *Calapooya Collage.* She has published two poetry chapbooks. She lives in Douglas, Alaska.

GINNIE GOULET GAVRIN

Charms

My mother wore jewelry that shined—
a gold chain whose clasp
was a delicate hand
reaching the way hands reach
in old valentines.

Every finger finely formed,
forever reaching for its clasp,
though strength was not at stake,
only holding, the way a mother lifts
her newborn's tiny fingers.
The way sentimental lovers
toy with touching,
a pleasure for the heart,
a pressure felt as tingling,
immune to argument,
one breath's leap
over the gasp of disappointment.

It was a hand that promised coupling,
joining that held fast and secure,
a hand worn at the throat,
as though to name the ache there,
a talisman and a warning—
the way jewels sparkle with their story:
opals for steadfastness,
rubies for passion,
diamonds for clarity.
Secrets coded in the angles
altering light
as we receive it on earth,
refracted,
a reassurance,
a dispersed answer to a prayer.

GINNIE GOULET GAVRIN lives in Marlborough, New Hampshire. Her short stories have appeared in the literary magazines *Thema* and *Primavera,* and she has just completed her first novel.

T. M. MOORE

Wyeth's Windows

IN TIME, SECULAR, MATERIAL CULTURES become infatuated with unseen worlds. We see it today not only in the curiosity about angels that is evident on television and in film, or in the seemingly endless new groups and religions springing up under the banner of New Age spirituality, but also in the fascination with bygone ages—the films of Jane Austen novels, television documentaries on the Civil War and Teddy Roosevelt, and faraway places, the speculations of astronomers and particle physicists concerning the ends of the universe and the nature of reality.

This is not unique to our age. Rather, it is inherent in the nature of man to pursue links with the past, with abstract ideas and emotions, and with spiritual realities. As Eugene Halton has observed, the urge for transcendence is basic to being human.[1] Or, more to the point, as Augustine wrote in his prayer to God, "thou has created us for thyself, and our heart cannot be quieted till it may find repose in thee."[2] The early scientists understood this—Newton, Descartes, Swedenborg, and others—and, in their writings, they moved easily between the material and spiritual worlds, their observations on the scientific realm provoking them to new and deeper meditations on the spiritual nature of reality.

Rather than look askance at what some might regard as the fantasizing of our age, we would be better advised to seek out the best sources, among the many clamoring for our attention, to help us gain insight into these unseen worlds, a function that art has always played in Western society. Jacques Barzun writes, "if art has importance, it is because it can shape the minds and emotions of man. It can enlarge or trivialize the imagination. If it can do so much, it affects the social fabric as well as individual lives for good and evil."[3] Art historian Leo Steinberg envisions art's social role of "fixating thought in aesthetic form, pinning down the most ethereal conceptions of the age in vital designs, and rendering them accessible to the apparatus of the sense."[4]

A contemporary artist whose popularity seems only to increase is Andrew Wyeth. Wyeth is identified with the Brandywine school of artists, so called for the Pennsylvania valley in which these artists lived (and live) and which commands so much attention in their paintings. The Brandywine school traces its lineage back to the early twentieth-century illustrator Howard Pyle and includes N.C. Wyeth (Andrew Wyeth's father), Jamie Wyeth (Andrew Wyeth's son), and a host of less well-known painters and sculptors. Brandywine artists are associated with a kind of natural realism that would appear to be out of step with the rank and file of contemporary interests. For, despite the very realistic images that fill his paintings, with these symbols Andrew Wyeth is describing unseen worlds that reflect our interest in matters of spirit. He himself says that he is primarily an abstract painter, more interested in capturing emotions than in merely portraying scenes from nature or depictions of country people so familiar to his native Chadds Ford, Pennsylvania, or the Maine coast around Cushing.[5] Like a poet, Wyeth uses everyday objects and common people to represent unseen worlds—a bucket becomes the dying Robin Hood, an old tree recalls the wounded General Lafayette, a woman's nude body evokes the promise of spring. Each of these unseen realities, in turn, calls up some emotion, as the symbols in Wyeth's paintings work to bring viewers together into what for him is the deeper, more vital world of human sentiment.

Windows feature prominently in many Wyeth paintings. Seen from all kinds of perspectives, sometimes alone, sometimes in groups, windows for Wyeth become a vehicle of transportation, projecting the viewer beyond the immediate setting into the past, the future, to death, or to other states of mind or being. Shuji Takahashi observes,

> The window physically divides inside from outside, represents the point of contact with a different world, and can be interpreted as a type of boundary. It can therefore be seen as a symbol of the division between the world after death, as indicated by the gazes of the figures portrayed, and the world of the living inhabited by the artist.[6]

Martha R. Severens sees Wyeth's windows as transparent openings that offer a view within, and often beyond.[7] Andrew Wyeth challenges us to go beyond the merely visible to imaginary worlds, the depths of human character, and bygone days, and to take delight, through the medium of simple things, in more sublime realities.

In *Wind from the Sea* the viewer is standing in a stark upstairs room in Christina and Alvaro Olson's house on the Maine coast, the only venue besides Chadds Ford that Wyeth has consistently painted. The artist has just entered the room, which had not been used for many years, and opened the window. A wind from the sea, just visible beyond the yard to the upper left on the horizon, lifts the tattered curtains and draws them up eerily, like billowing sails, revealing the lace sea birds delicately sown into the fabric. The present reality—the room—is plain, unadorned, even barren or trite, much as the lives of Christina and her brother Alvaro must have appeared to their neighbors. But not to Andrew Wyeth. Their Norwegian heritage evoked for Wyeth terrifying images of seafaring peoples, rugged men and women who made life work for them against the greatest odds. *Wind from the Sea* opens a window on that world for us, linking the Olsons with a romantic and fearsome past captured in the breeze, the hint of the ocean, the seabirds, and the billowing curtains. We are carried beyond the present into the past, beyond the feeble and commonplace to the terrifying and romantic, our imaginations thrilled by the prospect of former days, and our respect for the Olsons lifted like those tattered curtains to new heights of admiration.[8] Realizing their heritage, and appreciating their struggle to survive—Christina was a cripple and Alvaro single and retiring—we are filled with admiration, even awe, for this curious couple who made lives for themselves on the bleak Maine coast, and we begin to understand Wyeth's deep and abiding love for them.

Big Room also projects us into the past, but not unto heights of soaring admiration so much as to the gloom of sadness and loss. We are in Wyeth's childhood home, in the big room where the family gathered for Christmas each year and where Wyeth has many fond memories of playing with his toy soldiers in front of the Christmas tree, which would have stood just out of the picture to the right. We are facing the fireplace, but there is no fire. The room is empty, save for a pedestal table in the foreground, on which some fresh apples have been arranged. Light of a winter's afternoon is pouring through windows on either side of the fireplace, the beams traversing left to right across the painting to fall outside the picture, on the very place where the Christmas tree would have stood. A bust of Beethoven rests on one windowsill, its face (but not its features) unrecognizable. A clock stands on the mantle, its hands stopped at 10 minutes to 6 (which time it cannot possibly be, given the light outside in the midst of winter). Another version of this same scene carries the name, *Before Six.* Several faceless photographs are arranged to the right and left of the clock.

Although Wyeth's sister still lived in this home at the time of the painting, the big room had not been used for years.[9] Yet it was filled with warm memories of Wyeth's childhood, particularly of his father, the artist and illustrator N.C. Wyeth, who was killed in a train accident in 1945. Wyeth wants us to see that a significant part of his life had been taken away by the death of his father. He has incurred a tremendous loss, and he is filled with deep and abiding sadness, yet with fond memories of love and family at the same time. Everything in the room summons him to remember those happy days of his childhood, when his father was the animating figure of the family, especially at Christmas time. The sense of loss is palpable, even forty years later (the painting was completed in 1988)—faceless figures, time stopped in its tracks, the Christmas tree out of sight but not forgotten. They are so painful that they must be remembered: "There are some memories we relive over and over, as if we are trying to bear them."[10] And the light from the windows, together with the fresh apples on the table, at just about the place where the artist would have stood to paint this beautiful watercolor, and where we stand as we view it, remind us of our duty to suffer loss with dignity and grace, keeping our happy memories alive, even at the price of great pain.

Finally, *Evening at Kuerner* shows us a view of the farmhouse of Karl Kuerner, Wyeth's Chadds Ford neighbor and friend, a German immigrant whose life symbolized so much beauty and brutality for Wyeth. It is dusk, early in the spring. We can just see the buds beginning to appear on the trees in the background, and the ground is mushy from the cattle and the thawing of winter. Light emanates from a single window in the Kuerner house. Karl is inside, recovering from an illness that almost took his life. The light from the window is so bright that it illuminates the porch and the outside wall of the house, an effect created by allowing the natural white board to show through untouched. For Wyeth this window symbolizes hope, in particular the hope of spring and the recovery of his friend Karl.[11]

The return of spring, like the recovery of Karl, is reason to rejoice. Simple annual routines and the triumphs of life must not be taken for granted. We must take time to celebrate the hope that springs eternal all around us.

Andrew Wyeth uses windows to help us look into unseen worlds of history, past experiences, human character, and deep-seated emotion. They are a way of looking back, looking ahead, and looking within. By capturing his own sentiments so powerfully he invites us to share in a common experience, to come together over his paintings to enter an unseen world with him. Through Wyeth's windows we are led to look beyond the merely material world to the deeper, ultimately more real world of human emotion where, in spite of our many differences, all humanity meets on a common field.

Unseen worlds continue to beckon us. Even the very heavens above, the skies, the earth and all that is in them, call out to us, as both David and Paul remind us, to consider the glory of another realm and the nature of our connectedness thereunto.[12] Since we cannot escape this urge for something transcendent, and since there are so many voices claiming to point the way for us to connect with it, we must with great care and circumspection seek out the most reliable guides to the unseen worlds, those who can best help us to journey there.

T.M. MOORE is president of Chesapeake Theological Seminary in Baltimore, Maryland.

Notes

1. Eugene Halton. *Bereft of Reason.* University of Chicago Press, 1995. p. 114.
2. William Watts, trans. *St. Augustine's Confessions.* Cambridge: Harvard University Press, 1939. p. 3.
3. Jacques Barzun. *The Use and Abuse of Art.* Princeton University Press, 1975. p. 17.
4. David Levi Strauss. Rescuing Art from Modern Oblivion. *The Wilson Quarterly.* Summer 1997. p. 39.
5. Richard Merryman. Andrew Wyeth: An Interview. In Wanda M. Corn, ed. *The Art of Andrew Wyeth.* New York: Little, Brown, & Company, 1973. pp. 49, 53.
6. Shuji Takahashi. The Inner World of Andrew Wyeth. In *Aichi Prefectural Museum of Art: Andrew Wyeth Retrospective.* Nagoya, 1995. p. 257.
7. Martha R. Severens. Andrew Wyeth: America's Painter. In Martha R. Severens. *Andrew Wyeth: America's Painter.* New York: Hudson Hills Press, 1996. p. 17.
8. Andrew Snell, dir. *The Real World of Andrew Wyeth.* London Weekend / RM Productions, 1980.
9. Richard Merryman. *First Impressions: Andrew Wyeth.* New York: Harry N. Abrams, 1991. p. 26.
10. Barbara Drake. *Writing Poetry.* Ft. Worth: Harcourt Brace College Publishers, 1994. p. 25.
11. Thomas Hoving. *The Two Worlds of Andrew Wyeth: A Conversation with Andrew Wyeth.* Boston: Houghton Mifflin, 1978. p. 62.
12. Psalm 19.1–6; Romans. 1.18–20.

LINDA HOLT

St. Teresa and the Seven Chakras

THE SEVEN LEVELS OF CONSCIOUSNESS that lead to the highest state in which we experience God in all our actions and perceptions is one of the key concepts underlying Kundalini yoga. Kundalini is the life force—*chi,* breath of life—that pervades the universe and is released in an individual through various spiritual exercises, such as Kundalini yoga. Consciousness is raised by the sequential opening of the Seven Chakras. On a physical, and, some would argue, a symbolic level, the Chakras are perceived as nerve or energy clusters located along the spinal column, rising from the base of the spine to the crown of the skull. According to most schools of yoga, the Kundalini power or energy arises and flows upward in the spine as each cerebrospinal center unfolds over time through growing spiritual awareness. The Chakras often are depicted as lotus buds that blossom in many-petalled splendor, each more radiant than the last, culminating in an ineffable explosion of bliss as, at the Seventh Chakra, the individual self and the Divine Self become one.

Teresa of Avila, a Spanish mystic (1515–1582), advocated seven similar states of spiritual growth which were incorporated in her work *Interior Castle.* Teresa de Cepeda y Ahumada, later known as Teresa de Jesus, joined a monastery when she was twenty, devoting her life to prayer and God. Despite harassment by powerful church officials, in her later years she resolved to reform her monastery, which she felt had drifted from its original intention. In 1562 she opened a new monastery in Avila and later established seventeen

Leah Olivier.
Pen-and-ink, 1998.

houses of Carmelites. Teresa was canonized in 1622 and the first woman proclaimed a Doctor of the (Catholic) Church in 1970.

It would not have occurred to Teresa to use the spine as a metaphor for the seven spiritual states she described as the *moradas* or mansions within a mystical castle invisible to the world's eye. In the sixteenth century she lived in a world of castles, dusty churches, and medieval relics, and her idea of mansions undoubtedly originated from the New Testament: "In my house, there are many mansions. I go to prepare a place for you." Teresa uses the language of her religious tradition to outline a specific program of inner development which she guarantees will take each of her nuns, no matter how modest her abilities, to the state known in the East as Nirvana, *satori*, oneness with the Tao or nirvikalpaka *samadhi*.

Interior Castle is a guidebook for the soul. Few other spiritual leaders in either Eastern or Western traditions have spoken with such authority, assuredness, and conviction as to the efficacy of their path. While the imagery used to describe Chakras and Mansions may not match exactly, there are striking similarities between both paths, especially in the way they build from the depths of primitive consciousness to a state of sublime awareness. The seven states are outlined here starting at the root Chakra, Muladhara, which is associated with the earth, and culminating in the seventh or Sahasrara Chakra, which is best expressed in Meister Eckhart's words, "The eye by which I see God is the same eye by which God sees me."

First Chakra: Muladhara
(The Root or Earth Chakra)

THE LOWEST OF THE CHAKRAS, the first, is associated with the physical plane. Sometimes called the Earth Chakra, it is physically identified with basic anatomical functions such as elimination. On a vibratory level, it produces the slowest, densest vibrations, such as those of rocks and stones. It has a valued role as the foundation, the point of departure from which the spiritual journey takes off. The Kundalini is sometimes called "the serpent power"; it lies coiled and sleeping at this Chakra. When opened, the serpent stirs, and Muladhara results in awareness of the subtle forces at play in even the lowest forms of matter. According to Vishnudevananda, meditation on this Chakra brings steadiness to the body.

The first Mansion (Mansion of Humility) is the ground floor of the interior castle or soul. At this level, the primitive soul is tempted by what Teresa calls "snakes and vipers and poisonous creatures" lurking in the courtyard outside the castle, symbolic of sin in the Catholic religion, and the deceiving facade of *maya* in yoga. All is cold and dark in this spiritual basement, called the Mansion of Humility, where novices must spend a long time developing self-knowledge. As befits initial spiritual seekers everywhere, Teresa enjoins, "self-knowledge is so important that, even if you were raised right up to the heavens, I should like you never to relax your cultivation of it; so long as we are on this earth, nothing matters more to us than humility."

Second Chakra: Svadhisthana
(The Genital or Water Chakra)

AS THE BOOK OF GENESIS DESCRIBES THE CREATION, water followed earth, and so it is with Svadhisthana. At this level of consciousness, one becomes sensitive to the vibrations emanated by liquids, whether in bodies of water or within the body. This Chakra, physically represented near the genital area, is associated with sexual desires and has been called the Chakra of the animal self. The second

Chakra represents the point in consciousness where selfless love breaks away from, or evolves out of, selfish lust. The way we view the second Chakra is the source of much controversy in yoga. Some practitioners believe that the sexual impulse must be overcome if one is to rise to the third level of consciousness. Other yogis subscribe to the tantric school which uses physical experiences and objects as tools to advance on the path of knowledge. For them, the second Chakra is an opportunity to use sex as a vehicle for spiritual development. A contemporary view is that sex is neither an obstacle nor a path to knowledge, but rather a part of human nature. We examine our sexual nature dispassionately in the second Chakra and recognize it for what it is, no more. Then we are moved to the next plane as our consciousness is developed and enriched.

In the beginning was the Word, and for Teresa it is prayer (the Second Mansion or Mansion of the Practice of Prayer), which lifts the meditator into the next state of awareness. This is not the powerful Prayer of Union she practices in the Fifth Mansion still to come, but the humble prayer or japa of devotion which slowly but reliably lifts the spirit toward the Divine. Still susceptible to the poisonous influences of the world, the seeker moves slowly into mansions where warmth begins to spread and the light of truth dawns on the subconscious. Teresa was a woman of her time, and as such, would not describe the "animal self" in sexual terminology. Her use of speech as a metaphor, however, is appropriately parallel, for language is what distinguishes humanity from the other animals. What better way to transform animal utterances into tools for transcendence than through the language of prayer?

Third Chakra: Manipura
(Navel or Fire Chakra)

SWAMI RAMA HAS NOTED that there is a world of difference between the first two and the second two Chakras. The opening of the Third Chakra creates more energy, movement, and active involvement. Like the first step in Maslow's Hierarchy of Needs, the first two Chakras deal with our animal nature. The Third and Fourth Chakras teach us what it means to be fully human. Heat in all its manifestations—fire, light, warmth—is the element associated with Manipura. As this Chakra opens, one becomes attuned to the vibratory patterns of fire. Physically represented behind the navel, it is close to the lower *tan t'ien* of Taoist internal alchemy, the lower furnace in which the spiritual elixir is generated. Here we recognize, for the first time, that worldly attainments will not satisfy us.

In the Third Mansion (Mansion of Exemplary Life), Teresa recognizes that we are still enmeshed in the worldly life with its responsibilities and distractions. Following a path of good works, self-discipline, and vigor has enabled much progress, but there is far to go. Like a violinist who practices every day, we have mastered the fundamentals and play all the notes flawlessly, but we still aren't making music. What we lack is soul, a sense of vision: in a word, love.

Reason—so important in making the initial decision to follow the path of the spirit—stands between the seeker and the sought. It is as though the analytical and logical left side of the brain has been developed to the breaking point and hasn't yet burst through the barriers to the intuitive right side in which we start to experience knowledge of God.

Fourth Chakra: Anahata
(Heart or Air Chakra)

THE FIRST THREE CHAKRAS are characterized by a downward tendency. The spirit desires to regress back to the primitive level and falls sway to a kind of cosmic gravity which it must fight against in its ascent up the Chakra ladder. According to Swami Gnaneswarananda, at the fourth center, the psychic energy reverses itself, and, like incense rising naturally upward into still air, flows heavenward in both literal and figurative senses.

This Chakra is associated with respiration (pranayama, one of the eight limbs of yoga, is the science of using the breath to advance progress to the highest states of consciousness). Others link the opening of the Fourth Chakra with an affinity to air and all other gaseous substances, things which are real but often invisible, preparing us for the ultimate knowledge of a divine being who permeates all things but has no discernible form.

But perhaps most meaningful in drawing a comparison with the work of Teresa of Avila is the Chakra's popular representation as a blue, twelve-petalled lotus symbolizing the heart, omnipresent and all-embracing, the radiant devotion of the Bhakti yoga who sacrifices all at the feet of love.

In the Christian tradition, the greatest gift is love, and it is love which opens up the Fourth Mansion (Spiritual Consolations) for Teresa, one of the church's most passionately devotional saints. Rather than air, the metaphor of water appears: the spring of divine love nourishes and feeds the fountain of the soul. The barrier of worldly imprisonment—the too tight constrictions of the rigid, analytical life—breaks down, like a dam crushed in a roaring flood. One sees what is real, what is important, and, like the yogi whose fourth Chakra has blossomed in multi-petalled splendor, the first taste of Reality behind appearances occurs.

At this stage, however, total abandonment to divine love is not yet possible. Although we are no longer bound to the world in webs of delusion and desire, we fall back and forth between prayers, the Logos or Word of God, and ordinary consciousness. It is a stage of liberation, but also of frustration, for we see how far we have to progress, and our heart aches with yearning.

Fifth Chakra: Vishudha (Throat [Speech] or Ether)

OUT OF LOVE FLOWS PURE GOODNESS AND BEAUTY. The yogi who has experienced the unfolding of this Chakra is one with the cosmic ether, even beyond our planet and universe, and embodies the other-worldly qualities of clarity, omnipresence, and transcendence. The yogi hears and understands sounds too subtle for the ordinary human ear and experiences the vibrations of the universe on a very personal level. Because of these heightened states of sound and vibratory consciousness, the Fifth Chakra is associated with speech.

Like the Fifth Chakra, the Fifth Mansion (The Spiritual Betrothal and the Prayer of Union) opens up to us around the metaphor and use of speech. In Teresa's work, this is the Prayer of Union, the fervently expressed desire to attain the highest knowledge, union with the Beloved. "Oh, how much to be desired is this union!" she writes, "Happy the soul which has attained to it, for it will live peacefully both in this life and in the next as well."

Teresa's description of the Fifth Mansion also parallels Chakra literature in likening the soul to an earth-bound silkworm which is transformed into an airy butterfly in these rooms, and which has no wish but to rise higher and higher on the stream of spiritual development. She calls the seeker a "little dove," a common Christian symbol for the soul rising in knowledge and love. Like the yogis of India, she enjoins us to practice perfect love of our neighbor even as we pursue the self-cultivation for which we were born.

And grow we must, continuing through the Mansions and mastering their lessons until we reach the highest. "It is unthinkable," she writes, "that a soul which has arrived so far should cease to grow: love is never idle, so failure to advance would be a very bad sign. A soul which has once set out to be the bride of God Himself, and has already had converse with His Majesty and reached the point which has been described must not lie down and go to sleep again."

Sixth Chakra: Ajna (The Third Eye or Mind)

FOR MANY YOGIS, THIS IS THE ULTIMATE CHAKRA consciousness, the nerve center (which Yogananda ecumenically called the Christ

Consciousness) located between the eyebrows. Here the rising Kundalini finds full expression, where the three energies—*ida, pingala,* and *shushumna*—bloom in a kind of spiritual garden and form a sacred knot. One of its representations is an eye in a pyramid, a symbol common to both Hindu and Judaeo-Christian traditions. Mastery over the mind as well as matter occurs as the devotee experiences the opening of this mysterious portal to the soul.

At the Sixth Mansion (Seeing the Beloved), the seeker sees God, but not with the worldly eyes. "She was conscious that He was walking at her right hand, but this consciousness arose, not from those senses which tell us that another person is near us, but in another and a subtler way which is indescribable."

In a section of *Interior Castle* which is both complex and lengthy, Teresa compares the *satori* of sudden awakening to a flash of lightening, not unlike what is seen by the yogi during meditation on the Third Eye. "This most glorious image," she writes, "is so deeply engraven upon the imagination that I do not believe it can possibly disappear until it is where it can be enjoyed to all eternity." She cautions that it is not just a function of our physical body, but rather something that is really alive, speaking to the soul and revealing to it its mysteries.

Like the opening of the Sixth Chakra where the inner light, the blue pearl, and the precious diamond of wisdom are revealed, the Sixth Mansion opens its doors to the soul with a brilliance which Teresa likens to "a sun covered with some material of the transparency of a diamond, if such a thing could be woven."

Patanjali, the father of yoga, devotes many words in his sutras to the proliferation of visions which occur in deep meditation, warning against staying too long in their presence lest we never progress beyond them into real bliss. We can almost imagine Teresa nodding her assent to his advice. "[God] . . . reveals His love for us by means of such wonderful appearances and visions," she notes, but cautions that dwelling on them is a self-indulgence which makes true progress impossible.

In some ways the Sixth Mansion is as threatening as it is sublime. Here the soul has come so close to union with its Beloved, whose face she sees so clearly in the inner light, whose presence is so palpably near. The temptation is to yield to these sensations and progress no further. But for the seeker who has the interior strength to weather new distresses and challenges, the Seventh Mansion awaits, unutterable and absolute in its sublimity.

Seventh Chakra: Sahasrara
(Pure White Lotus, Brain, Consciousness)

THE THOUSAND PETALLED LOTUS OPENS, and the yogi experiences Self-realization which lifts him beyond the world of illusion. Here, the Kundalini merges with the Infinite in _samadhi_. The yogi sees that the world is what it has always been: ineffably ecstatic Oneness. But this divine unity, of which every soul is a living part, is clouded by the senses and rhythms of the material world. Beyond speech, beyond description, beyond comparison, the opening of the Seventh Chakra is something we can know only for ourselves.

Vishnudevananda points out that the Kundalini current will continue to descend and rise through the Seven Chakras time and again as the yogi vacillates between the waking state of samadhi and the somnolence of the world. "Only by long and continued practice," he writes, does this sakthi (power) make a permanent union, and the aspirant becomes a liberated soul. He is no longer bound or limited by time, space or causation, and all is joy and eternal bliss itself. He is immersed in the ocean of bliss and becomes the possessor of all knowledge and powers."

The Seventh Mansion (The Spiritual Marriage) is the culmination of the soul's quest on earth, for here is where the Spiritual Marriage between the soul and the Divine takes place. In this final Mansion, flooded with sublime light, the soul encounters and merges with the three persons of the Trinity. God removes the scales of illusion and ignorance which have veiled the seeker's eyes heretofore "so that what we hold by faith the soul may be said here to grasp by sight."

In consonance with the testimony of yogis for thousands of years, Teresa stresses that the soul does not stay fixed at this point but moves back into the world to serve humanity and God in humankind. In fact, like a Buddhist "Bodhisattva" who vows to defer enlightenment until all beings are saved, she emphasizes the importance of praying for, and otherwise aiding, those still enmeshed in the world of illusion and ignorance (or "sin," as it is called in the Christian tradition). Nor, despite the highest attainment, is the soul safe from the delusions of ordinary life. Teresa likens the Seventh Mansion to a palace inhabited by a great king while wars are waged throughout his kingdom. "But he remains where he is despite them all."

But despite these concerns and considerations, the illumination of the Seventh Mansion transports Teresa and the reader in some of the most beautiful and intelligent lines in mystical literature:

We might say that union is as if the ends of two wax candles were joined so that the light they give is one: the wicks and the wax and the light are all one; yet afterwards the one candle can be perfectly well separated from the other, and the candles become two again, or the wick may be withdrawn from the wax.

But here it is like rain falling from the heavens into a river or a spring; there is nothing but water there, and it is impossible to divide or separate the water belonging to the river from that which fell from the heavens. Or it is as if a tiny streamlet enters the sea, from which it finds no way of separating itself, or as if in a room there were two large windows through which the light streamed in: it enters in different places but it all becomes one.

Raptures, visions, uncertainties vanish as the soul enjoys its homecoming in the Source of all being.

Conclusion

FOR MANY CONTEMPORARY SEEKERS, all this talk of raptures and ecstasies, austerities and self-effacements, can be off-putting, not only in the work of Teresa and other Western mystics, but also in the scriptures, commentaries, and oral teachings of the East. Seekers of East and West alike sometimes abandon their own traditions for the other, putting a spiritual spin on the adage, "the grass is always greener."

Considering that Teresa would have had no knowledge of yogic tradition, it is striking to compare the commonality of spiritual pathways forged by gifted, inspired, and diligent seekers throughout history and around the world. Does this occur because the finite human brain is configured to think in only so many ways? Or is it because there *is* one path to Truth, like a network of separate tunnels leading to one luminous Hub?

Perhaps through the harmony of the Seven Mansions, Teresa discovered a form of Chakra consciousness, patterned step by step in the teachings of virtually every school of yoga. Look again at the courtyard before the First Mansions, filled with reptiles, amphibians, and poisonous creatures. There you'll see, coiled silently among them, the Serpent Power, ready to rise and lift the soul into Self-awareness, Chakra by Chakra, one Mansion at a time.

LINDA HOLT is a doctoral candidate at Drew University in Madison, New Jersey, and associate vice-president for college relations at Thomas Edison State College, a national leader in distance and experimental learning for adults. Author of a new transliteration of the yoga sutras of Patanjali, she has been widely published on the subject of yoga, Eastern thought, and spirituality. Her articles have appeared in *The New York Times, Liberal Education, Washington Times,* and other publications.

PERRY S. MARTIN

Homebody

Eleanor R. Searle,
Watercolor, 1997.

THE MUSIC, THE OLD SONGS, TAPES, AND MESSAGES are always with us. Like ghosts they haunt our bodies, eager to emerge in nostalgia, gratitude, rage, or depression. Nothing is thrown away.

Much of our early emotional experience is physical; it comes to us before we have words to express how we feel. How and when we are touched, or not touched, teach us our first lessons in relationships. William James pointed out that our body sensations precede our emotions. Think about it: you are driving peacefully along a winding road, and, as you round a curve, a car comes toward you too fast, too close. You respond with fear, grabbing your steering wheel and pulling your car onto the narrow shoulder. When the other car speeds on by, you may react to that drop in your stomach or tightness in your chest with anger, yelling at the driver, complaining about the narrowness of the road, or even blaming yourself for being less attentive. First the physical feeling happens, then the emotion.

"The body is a road map for the journey of healing and recovery. It can tell us where we have been, where we are, where we need to go, and how to get there," writes Clyde W. Ford.[1] Chronic unresolved issues often lie beneath chronic pain: our aches and pains have emotional roots.

Sigmund Freud stated that the ego is ultimately derived from bodily emotions. Wilhelm Reich concurred that manipulations of groups of muscles could bring into consciousness past memories and experiences held in the unconscious. He described the ways our bodies hold their old hurts, protectively developing what he called character armor to avoid painful emotions.

With the development of the neurosciences, we are learning how deep the connection is between our thoughts and our bodies. Through biofeedback we have seen that our mental state affects our physiological responses. Carl Simonton and Jeanne Achterberg showed that cancer patients could affect the course of their disease through the use of imagery. In her research with neuropeptides, Candace Pert has demonstrated that emotions are in the body as well as in the brain.

GROWING UP, we learned the rules for surviving in our family, though most of those rules were unspoken. Mine were relatively innocuous: *Don't ask questions—you'll be yelled at or teased.* So you always have to figure things out for yourself—and you'd better be right. What lodged in my chest and my throat and my shoulders was the fear and the shame that other people knew something I didn't know. As I grew toward puberty, I didn't ask questions about sex: the clear rule was, *Don't talk about it, and it won't happen.* I did not understand why my father screamed at my sister for her red nail polish and lipstick, or why she persisted in wearing them. I shrank into my body and felt small. At dancing school I was a wallflower, silent, sad, and unnoticed.

As I was growing up, I did not feel safe in letting my family members know how I felt. I did not ask questions or say what I thought. I physically shrank into my body, hunching to hide my small breasts. I learned not to speak unless I was positively correct, at home or at school. Symbolically, I gave up my voice. It became quiet and lodged in my throat. I was afraid to be seen and afraid to be heard.

So, much of my life I have lived in fear. One afternoon after a massage to quiet music, I opened my eyes and said, without any apparent thought, *There is nothing to be afraid of.* I learned this truth through safe and gentle touch. Without words, something that had contaminated my being for a long time was touched, then healed.

I WATCHED ILANA RUBENFELD WORK. Ilana is a long-time proponent of body–mind integration. Her client lay fully dressed on a massage table while she talked with him and touched his body lightly—head, feet, legs, hips, shoulders, arms. He began to open his life story to her and his heart to his wife who was present. Here was new "magic" I was determined to learn. Experiencing Ilana's work on my own body, I felt my shoulders soften and a new voice begin to sound. Ilana Rubenfeld, innovator in body–mind therapy, says,

> People store their memories and emotional reactions to their life experiences in ways that they're not usually aware of. If we try to present a good front, in spite of an experience having been toxic or traumatic, these feelings and the stress will show up in our bodies . . . One set of messages goes through the neocortex—the center of reasoning, language, and cognition—but the other comes through the limbic system and reptilian brain—the center of our emotional reactivity and survival instincts. Touch bypasses the neocortex and taps directly into the part of us that is driven by feelings. Through gentle touch, I try to help people listen to the emotional undercurrents of the experience that are frozen in the tissues of their bodies.[2]

As I pay attention to the right and left sides of my body, I feel differences that become metaphors: how when I always needed to be "right," I "left" out an intuitive creative part of myself. How, when I began to pay attention to and assert what was "right" for me, I often got "left" by my family. How when I am feeling "right," I may settle in, settle for less than I need to. In Rubenfeld Synergy therapy I discover that I can be fully balanced, in both sides of my body. I don't have to choose between right and left. My body feels more expansive and spacious, my shoulders wider. I take a firm stance and allow my breath to fill my whole self.

Working with the body as a Rubenfeld Synergist and psychotherapist, I guide my clients into opening to the symbols and symptoms and expressive images of their bodies with the goal of freeing their behavioral responses to the stresses of life. Margaret, talking about a family problem, feels her head cut off from the rest of her body, which she describes as "like concrete." As she lies on the table, I slip my hand under her hip, which she states feels heavy and lifeless. And, indeed, it does feel heavy to my touch. Bringing her awareness to the space between my hands, she images warmth and life returning. I feel the warmth and tingling in my hands. As we work together, feeling and life come back into her body, and she imagines a more colorful life for herself. She recognizes her own right to life and the choice she can make to stop carrying the weight of old family events around in her present life.

When children or adults experience physical or emotional abuse, they feel as if there is no safety in their lives. Sexual abuse leaves a lasting mark on the bodies of the survivors. Many who experience ongoing abuse learn to "go away," to absent themselves. They turn off from their bodies, vacating specific areas, going numb. Some even develop epileptic seizures. But the memories of the abuse are locked up in the body. As adults, these survivors often respond to pain through denial or simply not feeling. Sensitive work with their bodies can help them return to the reality of their kinesthetic senses and restore them to sensual and sexual pleasure.

When children's feelings are not taken seriously, they may grow up to invalidate their own desires. Monica works with giving herself permission to want what she wants, to recognize that not permitting herself the legitimacy of her desires actually impedes her from fulfilling her dreams. As she gets off the table, I leave the room to let an elderly client into the building. When I return, Monica is dancing around the room singing. "It's all right to want what I want." At our next meeting, she reports that her back which, unbeknownst to me, had been giving her trouble for some time, was feeling normal and resilient again.

Patrick, a mild-mannered man suffering from depression, began to cry as I touched his shoulder in his first session on the table: "I'm so angry and I'm afraid I'll hurt someone." He is furious at his dead father for his coldness. On reflection Patrick realizes he can't hurt his father now. He begins to tell his father how he failed, moves into yelling unprintable names, and then bursts into laughter. As he ended the session walking around the room, he marvels at the lightness of his body.

All of these events happened in the last two weeks. There is nothing extraordinary here. Each occurred because someone was listening to the body's story, listening with hands as well as ears. It is no more miraculous than a potter listening to a lump of clay spinning on the wheel as his hands assist it in becoming a cup or a bowl. Each piece of body–mind work creates a space where new choices for living become possible.

The challenge is to listen. There are many ways to unlock the symbols stored in our bodies. Meditation creates space. Proprioceptive Writing, developed by Linda Trichter Metcalf and Tobin Simon, is not just about writing, it is about listening to ourselves and writing what we hear. Massage, body therapy, holotropic breathwork, guided imagery with music, support groups, friends, or partners who will listen, all open the doors to inner perception.

Our bodies hold metaphors for exploring our lives. As I worked with Dan, I saw his right foot turned out and his left pointing straight ahead. Dan wants to start a new career; his right foot wants to stride out into new territory, but he is afraid to take a risk, to jeopardize his family finances. His left foot says, Let's just keep going the way we are; it's safe.

"The body is our instrument, the house we live in," says Ilana Rubenfeld, "and we need to listen to its song when we deal with emotional and spiritual issues."[3]

Moshe Feldenkrais developed exercises to help people's nervous systems release habitual holding patterns. F.M. Alexander, a Shakespearean actor from Australia, lost his voice, and in the process of curing himself, developed new ways of teaching posture with gentle touch, which release old holding blocks. Physical habit patterns can change when associated emotional material is processed. The body holds wisdom and truth, and psychological change, to be effective, has to be felt in the body.

Psychologist Eugene Gendlin works with what he calls a "felt sense"—a physical manifestation of feelings which connects to our bodily knowledge. As you focus on a feeling in your body—not trying to change it or get rid of it, simply observing it—you begin to experience a bodily shift, a change which may express itself in words that tell you what you need to do to respond to your feeling. Or the shift may bring images, maybe of some event in our past or of new possibilities for the future.

Experiments with hypnosis and sensory isolation, and therapies such as Jungian analysis, new-Reichian, Gestalt, psychosynthesis and guided imagery with music, as well as new forms of body-work, lead to deeper levels of consciousness. With the growing interest in the evolution of consciousness, we are no longer willing to be confined by the Newtonian–Cartesian mechanistic theories of the universe which we came to revere as "science."

Psychiatrist Stanislav Grof experimented with ways to break through to new levels of consciousness and found that his experiences could not be explained by science as we knew it. Grof, through the use of controlled breathing, evocative music, and focused body-work, led participants to what he called "nonordinary states of consciousness." He found them reliving elements of their biological birth with "astonishing verifiable" details. He suggested that the memories of these events and other traumas are contained in the tissues and cells of the body.[4]

Experiences with Grof's holotropic breath-work parallel the symbolism of death and rebirth from many cultures. Such transpersonal experience, which seems to be regressive in time, may be interpreted as re-incarnation or as connecting with what Carl Jung describes as archetypes of the collective unconscious, or as the Swedenborgian view of connection with spiritual "other world" states of being. These non-ordinary states of consciousness may come in the form of telepathy, psychic diagnosis, clairvoyance, or out-of-the-body experiences. Though they are accessed through the instrument of the body, they point to the reality that time and space are only superfluous constructs of the mind.

Our thoughts and our feelings are rooted in our physical existence. If you stop reading, close your eyes and say, "I remember," where do you go? What kind of feelings are associated with this memory? Did you feel strong or weak, heavy or light, short or tall, beautiful or unattractive? I remember the excitement in my throat upon reaching a mountaintop in New Hampshire, the deep contentment in my chest when I sit by my Maine lake. I remember how my stomach turned when my mother looked at me with disappointment in her brown eyes, how my shoulders froze when my father raged. I remember the smell of the barn in Indiana, the feeling of my hands when I milked the cows, and the sound of the milk squirting into the bucket. I remember how the raspberries tasted, picked on the hot sand dunes by Lake Michigan. Each memory grasped by my senses and held through the years, waiting for my return. And through these sensual memories I make meaning of mountains and lakes, of mother's expectations and father's fears, of farms and animals, and nature's bounty of summer berries.

This is my body, my home. When I listen, I learn to let go of the fear in my shoulders. When I walk I feel my feet touching the earth. Listening with my feet, I hear her pain. For we have abused our earth home as we have misused our own bodies, withholding the appreciation and care and respect this miracle of creation merits. We have exploited her resources, consuming her without tending to her needs for replenishment.

My hope for the children of the earth is that, in re-owning our bodies as precious gifts, we will also return to the earth the respect and care she deserves. This earth is also my body, my home, longing for tenderness, compassion, and love.

PERRY S. MARTIN is a psychotherapist and Rubenfeld Synergist, practicing at the Temenos Retreat Center in West Chester, Pennsylvania.

Notes

1. Clyde W. Ford. *Compassionate Touch.* New York: Simon & Schuster, 1993. p. 17.
2. Ilana Rubenfeld. Listening Hands. Interview by Richard Simon in *The Family Therapy Networker.* September–October 1997. p. 65.
3. Ilana Rubenfeld. *Changes Magazine,* June 1995. p. 33.
4. Stanislav Grof. *Beyond the Brain.* State University of New York Press, 1985. p. 36.

ANNE MCGINLEY

Where the Answers Are

Julie Reid.
Pen-and-ink drawing,
1998.

DAVID WOULD HAVE SAID I HAD A GIFT FOR SCIENCE. He liked to put things in spiritual terms. What I had was a great curiosity about the world. And since I loved the outdoors, a master's degree in wildlife biology was a natural. This was before anyone had even suggested wolves in Yellowstone, back when breeders had secretly released them in the Rockies. So when the university asked if I would spend two terms studying them, holed up in a cabin with some hermit—"He's harmless," they said—I knew I would get published. I geared up and went.

The hermit was David. He rose early every day. When I got up, a fire already snapped in the wood stove, coffee was made, and oatmeal was on the cook stove. He was a great cook, too. He made a Thai soup that was to die for. I remember the first night he cooked it. I sat at an old wooden table under the kitchen window, chopping dried hot peppers by lantern light. He wanted to know what I liked about my work at the university.

"When I'm cramming for finals I wonder that myself," I smiled, "but other times . . . I love to find answers to stuff. You know, to figure out how things work."

"Yeah," he said, stirring a big pot on the Coleman stove. "We humans are always looking for answers."

"Probably an endless quest." I put more peppers on the cutting board.

"You really want answers, though, I mean really the answers to everything, you won't find them out there." He gestured around the kitchen. "Nope. You find them in here." He pointed to his chest.

"What?" I joked, peering at the apron covering his chest. "You got wolves in there?"

David laughed, then shrugged. "Everything's in there."

I said nothing. I pushed back the kitchen curtains and looked out. They smelled dusty. Snow was falling hard. I would need my skis, maybe snowshoes, tomorrow.

Behind me, David said, "There are miracles in us all."

I turned. "I don't believe in miracles," I said. "Do you? Really?"

"Every day."

"I want tangible evidence." I rapped my knuckles on the table. "Something you can hold in your hands."

"Something you can hold in your hands," he said thoughtfully, then, "You like spicy food?"

"I do."

He nodded toward the pot. "This soup will be good for your throat."

I hadn't told him about my throat. Had I? "How did you know my throat hurts?"

"What do you think?" he grinned as though it were a great joke. "A miracle."

I went out every day to find the wolves. I was looking for individuals, since they wouldn't establish a den until later in the winter. For weeks I searched. We heard their howls creeping through the hours of half-light. I found fresh kills and followed their prints in the snow but would lose their trails when they shifted onto ice or along a ridge swept bare by wind.

At night, huddled under my pile of blankets, I would lie on my back and whisper, "I am finding the wolves by Friday." Then as the weeks went by and the days blended together I would say, "I'm finding wolves tomorrow." But I didn't.

Finally I couldn't drag myself out there again. For three days I hung around the cabin.

"If you're going to find the wolves you must become the wolf," David said to me the third night.

I was washing dishes. "Become the wolf."

"Yeah," he said. "You know what a wolf does? I mean their habits. Think about that and imitate them." He paused. "Look within yourself for the wolf."

"I don't want to be a wolf, Dave. I just want to see some." Then, hearing the sharpness in my voice, I said, "How about you go find them for me?"

He stood as though listening. "I'll go out with you tomorrow," he said finally. "But think now. You are a wolf, one of God's creatures." He got down on his hands and knees on the green tile floor. He crawled around for a minute, looking at the floor, then stopped and let out a pitiful whine. It was a very good imitation. I put a plate on the rack and turned to laugh with him. But his eyes had the same hungry look I'd seen in the eyes of captive wolves. I started; the skin on the back of my neck prickled. He whined again.

"David," I warned, "Don't get weird on me."

He sat back on his heels, smiling as though nothing had happened.

"You know," he said, standing up, "The Bella Coola Indians have a tale in which someone tried to turn all the animals into humans." He leaned toward me and half-whispered, "But with the wolves, the only part they succeeded in making human was the eyes."

The next morning, the sun sparkled on fresh snow. Together David and I silently snowshoed through the forest. About two miles from the cabin we came to a pearly-barked aspen grove, sheltered by a long ridge. I had been there many times.

"What do you think? You want to rest here and then head back?" I asked.

"Let's do." David looked wistfully around us. "This is a sacred place."

"Sacred?" I took off my pack. "You mean, like, to the Indians?"

David seemed to be listening to something. I looked at the trees for the first time: the shimmering aspens, the firs. "It is a nice spot. Beautiful."

I got out my camera bag and saw him watching. "Hey," I shrugged. "Got to do something with all that film I bought."

When I had taken some photos I looked around for David. His snowshoe prints led through the trees toward the ridge. I slung the camera strap around my neck and followed. At the base of the ridge, he had taken off his snowshoes and gone up. I left mine beside his and climbed after him.

At the top I heard David singing, or maybe chanting. The wind carried his voice to me in gusts. I crossed the ridge and saw him standing about 30 feet below, his back to me. And a wolf was slinking toward him through the trees.

At last! A wolf at last! This was the first time I had seen one in the wild, and my mind began to deliver data. Massive neck and shoulders, bunchy pelage, tufted leg fur. A male. At least 90 pounds; cannot immediately guess possible ancestry; fairly well fed.

But he was going for David. His body seemed to float over the lanky legs toward my friend—who simply stood there, the back of his head moving as he sang.

"David," I warned. The wind tossed my words back over my shoulder.

The wolf was big. David reached out his fist, fingers down, and held it there. He seemed to be saying something now.

"It's not a dog," I said, then shouted, "David!" The wolf startled, jumped away at my voice. But David spoke again. The wolf circled and slowly crept to him, then lunged upward and put his paws on David's chest. David tumbled to the snow and the wolf bounded away like a puppy. I heard laughter as I struggled with shaking hands to get the lens cap off my camera.

I took some of my best photos that day, of David and the wolf. Not long after that, I located a den. My work had finally begun.

For three months I gathered fine behavioral data. There were six individuals in the pack, each with a distinct personality. They were playful, even affectionate with each other. The weather began warming. Spring term was almost over.

When I think now about that last night, I think he must have known. I was packing my notebooks and said, "Look at this, David. Look at all this material for my dissertation. Now this," I pointed both index fingers at the box and grinned. "This is a miracle."

He looked surprised. "You think . . . ?"

"No. I'm just joking, silly."

David was thoughtful. "Every spring when I see a flower blooming in the snow I think that's a miracle," he said. "The love of two friends is a miracle."

"I'm . . ." I adjusted a notebook. "I'll miss you, Dave."

"We'll see each other again," he told me.

"Now all I've got to do is go back and do the writing and two more classes, and I'll be done. Done!"

"That will be good," he said. "I'm finishing up, too."

The next morning I went to the ridge overlooking the den. The day before, the sun had softened the snow; but it had frozen overnight to a hard, slick sheet. Footing was so treacherous I ended up crawling to the top on hands and knees.

I sat on a log that was perched right on the edge of the drop-off. As I rested I saw the beta female chasing a snowshoe hare. I got my camera and zoom lens out. The slope below was too steep for many trees to grow, so I had a clear view. But my snow pants were caught on a piece of bark. I twisted impatiently, refocusing, and snapped one picture, two . . . I yanked my leg to turn and it suddenly tore free. I hurtled off the log and over the edge.

I sailed down the ice toward the trees below, gathering speed, and heard a sickening snap when I hit. Then felt the screaming pain. When I looked down I could see my shin bone, torn right through my pants, the steaming blood already soaked up to my knee. I remember thinking about hypothermia, about the smell of blood and the wolves before I fainted.

When I awoke I was in my bed. I was in my T-shirt. I stretched, sat up and looked out the window at an overcast morning. Then I remembered. I flung back the covers. My leg was fine, of course it was. It must have been a nightmare.

I dressed in the freezing cabin air and went into a dark living room. David was lying on the couch, asleep in his checked flannel shirt and corduroys.

As I lit a lantern and built a fire in the wood stove the dream stayed with me. I made coffee and Wheat Hearts and went to peer at David. By the lantern light his skin was thin and pale. It almost seemed lit from within.

"David?" I said quietly. "Breakfast." He didn't stir. I gently shook his shoulder. Even through the shirt I could feel he was burning hot. "Oh shit," I said.

I called Search and Rescue. Told them he was really sick. They would have to truck snowmobiles up the highway and make their way up in the snow from there.

"David," I said, "just hold on, okay? They'll be here in maybe three hours and then we can get you to a doctor. You'll be fine." I was worried he wouldn't be fine, though. I didn't know what to do with a fever. I didn't know what was wrong. The morning went on and on with no sign of the snowmobiles.

I told him again that he'd be fine.

"Don't worry, Anne," he said, gentle as ever. "I'm always with you." Then he looked right beside me with that odd listening expression of his. I shivered and looked too, glanced around the room. Nothing was there.

"No!" he said, "Not me. She's the one. Yeah, her." He smiled at me.

Finally the paramedics came. On the landing behind the cabin they bundled him up and strapped him onto a sled.

I squatted beside him. "Hey, buddy, they messed your hair up. Can't let that happen." I smoothed it under his helmet. "That's better. Now, you're going to be fine," I told him. "One of these guys is waiting to give me a ride. I'm just going to get my stuff together, and I'll see you in town tonight." He nodded.

The driver came. I stood up. Now that the paramedics had him, I wanted to cry.

The engines roared, and they took off in a cloud of exhaust, pulling him slowly across the snow.

The man who had stayed came around a corner of the cabin. "What's this?" he called to me, pointing behind him. "Did he have an injury?"

"No," I said. "I don't think so."

"Who did? Did you?"

"What?"

"What is this?" he gestured impatiently. "Over here."

I followed him around the cabin. A set of bloody prints frozen in the snow. A pair of snow pants, covered with now-brown blood.

"Looks like a wounded animal was here," the man said. "Do you have a dog?" I reached for my leg. It was smooth and warm and perfect. I doubled over, ran my hand over the entire length of my pants.

He kept talking, asking me questions. "Look!" I said suddenly. I bent down beside the mess, there where the snow had melted. "Can you believe it?" With one finger I caressed a tiny green flower bud waiting to open.

ANNE MCGINLEY lives with her husband and two children in Eugene, Oregon, where she is writing her first children's novel.

STEVEN CARTWRIGHT

Neighborhood Watch

DID HE HEAR GLASS BREAKING OUTSIDE IN THE DARK? Emmett Nagel hobbled to the window, his cane prodding the carpet. He pulled the draperies back and stared into the gloom. It took a second for his eyes to adjust, but now he could see the circle of light cast by the street-light. And something else. His neighbor's house was only ten feet away, and he could see two teenage boys reaching into a lighted window. One of them pulled something out, and they turned and ran.

Emmitt turned away from the window and hobbled to the fridge. Opening the door, he reached in and removed a cold brown bottle.

Back in his faded lounge chair, in the den, his bad leg propped atop his favorite worn footstool, Emmett gulped his cold beer. As he watched one of his favorite movies, *It's a Wonderful Life,* he was soon awash in a warm, drunken glow.

Suddenly the drunken glow was a bonfire in his right knee catching his body on fire with pain. For a second he thought he was dying. He jerked and realized he had only been asleep; it was now morning.

"Can you get that?" Judith called from the beadroom, sleep still in her voice.

"Get what?" he barked, twisting in his chair.

The doorbell rang.

"It's only eight," she called, "who could it be?"

Emmett pushed himself up and stumbled for the front door. As he opened it, the cheery morning light hurt his eyes.

"Excuse me for disturbing you, sir," said a young man with close cropped black hair. In his hand was a badge that Emmett immediately recognized. "I'm Detective Cunningham. With the police department. There was a burglary last night at the Goldhagens'." I'm canvassing the neighborhood. To see if anybody saw anything last night. Around two in the morning?"

Emmett grumbled, "Come inside."

Detective Cunningham walked in, looking around.

"You work Burglary? Here, sit here, Cunningham, I gotta get off this leg."

Sitting on the green sofa, the detective drew a pad and pen from his vest pocket. "Can I have your name, sir?"

"I asked if you work Burglary. My name is Nagel. Emmett Nagel. Ever heard of me?"

The thirtyish detective shook his head. "Should I?"

"You assigned to Burglary?"

"No, sir. I work the Special Investigations Squad."

Falling into his lounge chair, Emmett cocked an eyebrow. "SIS, huh?" It was Cummingham's turn to cock an eyebrow, but he remained silent as he scrutinized the man sitting across from him, wearing a plaid housecoat cinched in the middle, blue pajama pants protruding, and brown bedroom slippers.

Emmett pulled his stiff right leg onto the padded footstool. "So you don't recognize my name? Well, why should you? The shooting's been five years ago now." At the word *shooting*, the young detective froze. "What about Troy Kincaid? You recognize *that* name, Cunningham?" Emmett laughed when he saw the cop's face go blank. "Relax, Cunningham. I used to *be* a cop. I never was a detective, just a beat cop because I loved the street. Even after twenty years, all the garbage I saw out there hadn't burned me out like it does most of us. I was still gungho, boy! That's why I rushed to that liquor store when I heard the thirty-six come up on the radio. Got there in time to see a man run out of the store wearing a ski mask, toting a bag in one hand and a .357 in the other. I shouted for him to freeze. The bastard froze for a second, then shot me. Blew out my whole damn knee." Emmett slapped the metal knee with dark glee. "He aimed right for my knee, but I shot to kill. And I did." His face was a scowl. "I killed the perp."

Cunningham looked startled. "Troy Kincaid?"

"Right. A fellow cop gone bad, robbing a liquor store."

"I'm sorry. I didn't connect your name, sir. I feel pretty stupid." He eased his body, began tapping his pen on his knee, comfortable now, one cop talking to a fellow cop. "I worked the morning watch when that happened. I'd only been on the department less than a year. I don't think I knew either of you guys. On a department of over a thousand . . ."

"Forget it, Cunningham. My buddies supported me through all my surgeries. After a while only my closest personal friends on the department still called or came by. Now there's only one who gives a hoot about me as I sit here and vegetate." Emmett forced a chortle. "Don't ever get yourself disabled, Cunningham. The world just passes you by."

"I'm sorry, Nagel—"

Shifting uncomfortably, Emmett blurted out: "I'm not looking for sympathy, Cunningham. I just wanted to let you know who you were talking to is all. Now, what about the burglary?"

The young detective grinned uncomfortably. "This morning around two, your neighbors—the Goldhagens—heard glass breaking in the front of their house. Do you know the Goldhagens?"

"I've seen but never met 'em."

"A young couple with two young kids. Her old man lives with them. He's kinda frail. He'd been a Holocaust prisoner."

"So they've decided that this was a bias crime? That's why someone from SIS, not Burglary, is working it?"

"Right. The burglar or burglars broke a window, and the only thing they stole was the Goldhagens' menorah."

"What's a menorah?"

"It's a nine-branched candelabrum used during the Hanukkah season. Electric candles. The burglar or burglars stole it. Beat officer found it a few blocks away thrown in a field. They had pulverized it and painted it black."

"Yeah, that sounds like the perps did it because the victims are Jewish. They're the only Jews in this neighborhood. Only been here a few weeks."

"Perps?"

"Huh?"

"You said perps, not perp. Did you see them, Nagel?"

Emmett shifted uncomfortably.

"Well?"

"Last night, around two, I heard something outside. Could have been breaking glass, no way to tell."

"Did you look outside?"

"It was dark."

"But you did look out?"

"Yeah, Cunningham. I looked out. But it was dark."

"So you didn't see the perps?"

"I may have seen something."

"The perps?"

"It was dark!"

"So you wouldn't be able to give me their description?"

Looking away, his shoulders sinking like a defenseless old man's, Emmett muttered: "I told you it was dark, Cunningham."

"I won't bother you anymore, Nagel," he said, rising to his full six-feet. "I can see you're in pain. But it's been nice to meet you. I recall now hearing some good things about you when you were on the street." He leaned down, extending his hand.

"You're lying. You haven't heard anything about me. It's too far in the past." He shook the young detective's hand anyway.

The front door closed behind the detective, and Judith walked in wearing a pink housecoat. "I didn't want to come in looking like this," she said, stopping a good ten feet from her husband, "but I heard what the detective said. It's horrible. People these days have no respect for others."

"Just kids," Emmett muttered, shifting in his chair.

"Kids? Then you did see them, Emmett?"

Scowling, shifting around again, he exclaimed: "I don't know *what* I saw, Judith. It was dark. I'd been drinking."

"Of course you had."

"And what's that little remark supposed to mean?"

Judith didn't answer but leaned down and began collecting the empty beer bottles around Emmett's chair. When she had all she could carry, she turned and walked toward the kitchen.

"They're the only Jews in the neighborhood," he called to her. "Why couldn't they move into one of their *own* neighborhoods? There's plenty enough of them on the northside!"

Judith came back and collected the last empty bottles and walked toward the kitchen again.

"Well," she said quietly, "I'm going to visit them."

"Visit *who?*"

"The neighbors. Didn't that detective say their name was Goldhagen? They have two small children and her sick father?"

"Why do you want to go visit them, Judith? Leave them alone. They'll be cleaning up the mess. Leave them alone, Judith."

Yet when she came back in the room she had put on a simple cotton dress, still no makeup, but he thought she still looked good enough without makeup. "What about breakfast?"

"You're not an invalid, even though you want everybody to treat you like one."

The front door shut behind her.

EMMETT SAT WATCHING MORNING TV, clicking from channel to channel. Judith seemed to have been gone an hour. Emmett fought to stand up, finally teetering on his cane, and hobbled into the kitchen. Searching the refrigerator, he grabbed a pack of cinnamon rolls and carried them to the breakfast table, throwing them down before returning to the fridge for a carton of milk. He ate two cakes cold and drank the milk from the carton. As he dropped a crumpled paper napkin onto the graveyard of empty beer bottles, the back door flew open. Judith hustled in, smelling of fresh morning air, but crying.

"What's wrong now?" Emmett muttered.

Judith was carrying a plastic grocery bag, and when she plunked it onto the table, it made a clanking noise. "What you got there, Judith?"

"They have the most adorable children."

"Who?"

"And the old man was in a Nazi prison camp. He's got this number tattooed on his hand. The Nazis did it for identification."

"You must be babbling about the Goldfarbs."

"*Goldhagens.* I swear, Emmett Nagel, you didn't used to be this bitter." Her tears flowed. "I know you saw horrible things on the department, and it was bad enough getting shot and disabled, and by a fellow officer, but—when I looked into that old man's eyes, there was so much pain. Nazis killed his wife and their son. And then some stupid vandals do *this*. I just wanted to do something. To show them we care, that everyone in this neighborhood isn't like those cowards last night."

Emmett extended his hand toward her, then dropped it to his lap and looked away. He sighed. "What's in the grocery bag?"

"I'm going to light it—plug it in, I mean—and put it in our window."

"Light it? What is it? A Christmas candle?"

His wife peeled the plastic sack back and Emmett looked blankly at the metal object. "What is that thing?"

"A menorah. What those vandals last night stole from the Goldhagens."

"And you want to put that thing in *our* window? Judith. We're Baptists, not Jews."

"It doesn't matter, Emmett. I'm doing it as a show of respect." Before he could say another word, she grabbed the electric candelabrum and left the room.

THE DAY PROGRESSED FOR EMMETT NAGEL as did all his days. Beer followed beer as he sat in his lounge chair before the tube, his right hand growing stronger from all the squeezing he did with the remote.

But the beer and the painkillers could never quite numb the pain. His metal knee seemed to suddenly turn into a machine gun, spewing bullets into every joint of his body. He wanted to lash out. Then he heard Judith call him from somewhere outside.

"Come here, Emmett! I want you to see this! It's marvelous!"

Muttering swear words, he fought to stand up, then clambered on his cane to the front porch. He stopped and looked out into the darkness. Couldn't see his wife. "Judith? What are you doing out there?"

"Come and see this, Emmett!" Her voice sounded rapturous, lyrical. He hadn't heard his wife this happy in . . . a very long time.

His eyes adjusted to the darkness, and he could see her standing in the Goldhagens' yard. He recognized the young couple, saw the two kids and the old man standing thin and slightly hunched over. "Judith, I can't walk all the way over to you. I could fall. What are you yelling about?"

"Look around you, Emmett. Don't you see all of them?"

"All of what, Judith?"

She swept her right arm in a slow arc, like a ballerina taking a bow. Emmett saw neighbors standing in their yards. What could make them all come out like this? Was there a house on fire? Everyone was out beneath the stars.

Then he saw the fires. Not house fires, but in every window of every house in the neighborhood, nine-branched menorahs blazed.

Emmett stumbled forward, mesmerized by all the dancing electric flames. Before he knew it, he was standing next to Judith and the Goldhagens. They, too, were looking at all the windows.

"The other neighbors saw our menorah in our window, Emmett, and they all went out and bought their own. Dozens and dozens of them, and it took a while for them to find out where to buy menorahs. Just look at all of them!"

EMMETT TURNED AND SAW THE OLD, HUNCHED MAN looking at him, and Emmett felt as though those eyes were drawing him in, into their own world of sorrow and loss. With a thick accent, the old man, a tear escaping one eye, said to Emmett: "Isn't it so beautiful, my friend?"

Something struck Emmett deeply, deeper even than the pain in his knee. He began crying, then sobbing, his big shoulders quaking. With his free hand, Emmett covered his red face, sobbing so profoundly he gasped for air. Judith and the Goldhagens quickly surrounded him,

comforting him,
soothing him,
slowly returning him to life.

STEVEN CARTWRIGHT, a veteran detective with the Atlanta police department, was previously a newspaper reporter and is an Atlanta native. He is now a free-lance writer, who also draws cartoons and illustrations, such as the two drawings he has made for this article.

PART II

Interlocking Stitches

Mementos We Hold

WE OFTEN CHERISH FAMILIAR SYMBOLS
through which we sometimes see things
we have not seen or dreamed before,
but sometimes we see only darkness
(as when traditional Christian symbols,
like the wise men at the manger,
lose their power).
The truth or fiction of the symbols themselves is irrelevant
in comparison to the truth of what they symbolize
(as with the provenance of The Shroud
or a memory of a certain friend).

In the same way, there is no right or wrong reality
to be seen through any particular symbol:
a manicured lawn can represent
an artistic ideal *and* a service rendered;
like buttons on a shirt,
rituals have the integrity of use.
Paul and Eng-li had the good fortune
to marry in the Year of the Dragon.

—ROBERT H. KIRVEN

TONIA TRIEBWASSER

Interlocking Stitches

My son is dead.
I grieve with needle
And thread,
Refilling a thousand thimbles
Of protesting tears.

Scissors sharpened in my lap.
Bolts of fabric
Unfurled,
Half-mast across the floor.

His wife has remarried.
His children cannot see me.

I am old.
Not dull.
I know where they live.
I keep track.
In the time of their growing,
I have seamed my missing
Into spring dresses.
Winter shirts,
Vests,
Slips,
A dozen quilts,
All graduating in size.
I fold them in a box,
Send them in the mail
Without a card.

TONIA TRIEBWASSER is a native Californian. She lives with her family in the foothills of northern California.

FREDRICK ZYDEK

Contemplating the Shroud

This is not simple cloth,
a mere remnant of threads
spun from sheep's wool,
honest cotton. These strands
weave the fibers of history.

Full as words, the cloth stirs
from the imprint of his hands,
the etched image of his arms,
folded here like fragile wings
trying to hold in the sun.

I search filaments for the web
of faith. I want the evidence
of things hoped for—things not
seen so much as prayed for, things
that want me to understand them.

It is said that when the moment
came, such a fire warmed his
sweat and grime it clung here,
a gift towards which the dead
might turn their resurrected gaze.

FREDRICK ZYDEK is the author of four collections of poetry: *Lights along the Missouri* (1976), *Storm Warning* (1983), *Ending the Fast* (1985), and *The Abbey Poems*, (1994; 2d ed., 1998). His work appears in *The Antioch Review, The Hollins Critic, Michigan Quarterly Review, Poetry, Poetry Northwest,* and other journals. Formerly a professor of creative writing and theology at the University of Nebraska and later at the College of Saint Mary, he is now a gentleman farmer when not writing.

Pretend Friends

I FIRST MET POLLY ON THE HILLSIDE. I asked her where she lived. She pointed down the road. There was no house anywhere near, just a tumbled-down pile of charred logs, overgrown with weeds and tag alders. With forest all around, I thought, perhaps a little Hansel and Gretel cottage might be hidden away in a clearing.

"Bonnie!"

Mummy was calling from her folding chair on the front porch.

Polly gazed at me with eyes too big for her thin white face.

"I have to go now," I said. "See you tomorrow."

She lifted one tiny hand in a wave. I ran back toward the house. Halfway there, I looked over my shoulder, but she had vanished.

Over my baked beans, I told Mum all about my new friend. She listened, her smile growing wider by the minute. "How old is this little girl?"

"Six, like me."

"Does she look like you?"

"She's taller but skinny. She has a mark on her neck."

Mum refilled my glass with tomato juice. "Is her hair brown, like yours?"

"It's gold, like princesses in my storybook."

"Is your friend a princess?"

"Of course not," Mummy. "What would a princess be doing up here in the bush?"

"Up there in the bush," was an expression Grandma had used. "It's foolish, following Bruce there," she said to Mummy before we left Toronto. "What will you do with yourself while he's out collecting ore samples? You and the child will be alone in the wilderness."

"It will be an adventure." Mummy calmly folded our clothes into a suitcase. "We'll be living in a perfectly good furnished farmhouse."

The house, rented sight unseen by Daddy from a real estate agent, may once have been perfectly good but had recently been a

Jessie Wilcox Smith. *Twinkle, Twinkle Little Star.* 1910. From a *Child's Book of Old Verses,* written and illustrated by Jessie Wilcox Smith. Library of Congress. Washington, D.C.

playground for mice, and the furniture was sparse, rickety, and peeling. On first stepping inside, Mummy took a deep breath, but all she said was that a little cleaning was required. She sent me out to gather some flowers for the table. Out on the hillside, picking daisies, I met Polly.

NOW MUMMY LOOKED AT ME WITH ONE EYEBROW RAISED. "Is your little friend's father a geologist, like yours?"

Sipping my juice, I thought for a moment.

"He's a farmer. Or maybe a hunter, like in the song." I began to sing, *In a Cabin in the Wood.*

Mummy applauded. "Nicely sung. Now, it's naptime. I'll read you *Old Mr. Toad.* Are you sure you saw a little girl? Maybe it was that big toad we saw under the leaves yesterday."

"It was a girl. Her name is Polly."

I drifted off to the familiar story and slept all afternoon, waking to my parents' voices.

"Bruce, it's hilarious. Bonnie has the most vivid imagination. She made up a story about this imaginary pal, using bits and pieces of the little songs and stories she loves so much. The pretend friend is Polly, like the song *Polly Wolly Doodle.* Polly's father is either a farmer, like *The Farmer in the Dell,* or a hunter, as in the song about the rabbit."

I ran out to the main room.

"Polly isn't just pretend," I told them loudly. "She's real."

"Well, if it isn't our little girl, wide awake." Dad held out his arms. "What did you do today?"

"Saw the toad under the back step. Picked dandelions. Played with Polly." Dad exchanged a glance with Mummy.

"Well, I collected some interesting ore samples that should please the company." Daddy lifted me into my chair at the supper table. As my parents talked, I ate, wishing I could give some food to Polly. She was so thin.

I wanted to give her some clothes, too. Hers were no good for playing. She didn't have any shoes. The pine needles, stones, and sharp blades of grass would hurt bare feet. Even in May, you needed a warm, zippered jacket like mine, and all she had was a white home-knit fraying sweater atop a faded yellow cotton dress with a too-long skirt. Only the buttons were pretty—pearls, like those on Mummy's angora sweater.

I didn't feel ready for bed at 7:30, so Mum and Dad and I played games of *Fish* and *Old Maid.* My parents spoke of their Saturday trip to town for groceries, more library books for Mum, and perhaps a movie at the Palace Theatre on Main Street. *The Kettle Family* was showing.

"May I invite Polly?" I looked up at my parents.

Mummy gave a little sigh.

"Why not?" Daddy said. But the following day when Mum was reading on the porch, I met Polly by the edge of the grove, and she said she couldn't come to town with us.

"Why not?"

"I can't. I have to stay here." That was no answer. It was like Mummy saying "Because," when I questioned something. So then Polly showed me where a groundhog was raising her babies deep in the earth beneath the pine-tree roots. Next we made daisy chains. As the sun rose in the sky, I started to get hungry. Smoke rose from our chimney, and I knew Mummy would be heating vegetable soup. I looked at my pale companion.

"Come for lunch with me." She shook her head.

"Come on. It will make your hair glossy and put roses in your cheeks." Mummy sometimes said these words to encourage me to eat. Now, observing Polly's lank hair and pallor, I understood what she meant.

"No. I can't. That's Grandma and Grandpa's house. I'm not allowed there. Grandpa said." Her eyes were two hazy pools. Her voice was the loneliest thing I had ever heard, except for the wolves howling at night.

"We live in the house over there, for the summer," I told her. "You can come. We've fixed it up, but we have no TV. No *Howdy Doody*. No *Gunsmoke*."

She looked mystified. "What's TV?"

"Television." She looked blank.

"Bonnie! Dinner!" My mother's voice was faint in the distance.

"I have to go now. 'Bye. See you." Polly nodded and disappeared into the grove.

Inside, I told Mummy that Polly had never seen television. "And I've never seen Polly." Her eyes met mine the way they did when she suspected me of lying and wanted the truth. "Maybe this afternoon before your nap, we can go out for a walk, and you can introduce me to Polly." She expected me to hesitate, but I was elated. "I will!" Bending my head over my bowl, I gobbled my food.

Mummy held my hand as we walked down the field to the grove. Purple vetch, white ox-eye daisies, and red clover brushed the legs of our jeans. Birds twittered in the leaves overhead, and a groundhog hurried to its burrow. "Polly!" I called. "Polly. We're here."

She was nowhere to be seen. Only our daisy chains remained, drooping in the sun. I picked them up and held them out to my mother. "See. This is Polly's and this is mine."

"Bonnie, how lovely!" Mummy bent to examine my handiwork. "I didn't know your little hands were so dextrous."

"Polly showed me how."

Mummy patted my head. "Or maybe you made one for yourself and one for Polly." I shook my head. She shrugged.

"There she is!" A flash of yellow caught my eye, but it was only a wild canary lighting on a tree at the edge of the forest.

"I don't think we'll see her today," Mummy said. That night I woke and stared at the moon beaming down. From behind my room's thin partition, I heard voices.

"I'm wondering if my mother was right about bringing Bonnie here," Mummy was saying. "She seems obsessed with this imaginary chum. Maybe she misses her friends and had to create one out of thin air. Maybe she misses TV. Today she told me Polly has never seen television."

"Bonnie seems happy." Dad's voice rumbled thoughtfully, "I hate to think of your going back home, Laura. It's wonderful to have a home to come to at night. But if it's getting to you . . ."

"Oh, I love it, so quiet, so close to nature, no standards to keep up. I like reading and enjoying the scenery. And I thought it would be healthy for Bonnie—the out of doors . . ."

"All kids go through a stage of having imaginary companions." Dad's sounded reassuring. "My pretend buddy was Hopalong, and whenever anything got broken or spilled, it was always Hoppy who did it." Mum laughed. I drifted back to sleep, feeling frustrated.

The following morning was cloudy. Mummy had my crayons and paper out and ready at the end of the table.

"The radio says there's a 70-percent chance of rain," she told me, as she stirred my porridge. "It'll be an indoor day." I climbed on a chair and looked out. In the mist I could see a slender figure in white by the pine, staring at the house.

"But I have to go out. Polly is waiting for me."

"Don't be silly, Bonnie. Sit down with your crayons."

"But I see her there."

Mummy didn't even bother looking. She pressed her hand to her forehead. "Bonnie, sit down at the table right now."

I ate, listening to the songs, to the news on the battery radio. Mummy swallowed an aspirin with her tea and began a letter to Grandma. I peeked through the window at Polly. She had ventured away from the tree and was closer to the house than ever before. She waved at me. I hoped she would come and knock on the door and have some porridge, but she just stood there.

After breakfast, I colored and drew, as Mummy did the dishes. "I have the most awful headache," she said. "I'll have to lie down." She left the door open so I could see her there with a wet washcloth over her eyes. After awhile, I could tell from her regular breathing that she was asleep. I looked out and saw that Polly had retreated to the pine tree. Carefully, soundlessly I crept out, ran across the gravel drive-way, and up the field through the tall grass toward my friend.

Her thin face lit up at the sight of me. "I thought you were nev-er coming," she said.

I pointed to the grey sky overhead. The mist in the valley and at the forest fringes had not cleared as it usually did. "I guess your mummy doesn't worry about the weather," I said.

To my surprise, tears welled up in her eyes. "What's wrong?" I reached for her bony hand.

She shook her head, weeping silently. I put my arm around her thin shoulders. "Where do you live?" If she was upset, she might want to go home to her mother. She pointed to the foggy edge of the forest.

"Come with me," she pleaded. Something made me draw away and I glanced at our house. Mummy would be worried if she woke and found me missing.

"I'm not supposed to," I said. Polly turned and began to run soundlessly through the weeds. "Wait!" I started after her, swishing through the daisies and timothy, pulling her dress. Then my foot caught in a tangle of vetch and I belly-flopped. Struggling to my feet, I saw her vanish into the haze. But what was it gleaming up from the dandelion leaves? A pearl button from her dress. Clutching it, I start-ed for the house as the first raindrops fell.

I was out of breath and crying when Mummy met me at the door.

"Where were you?"

"Just up the field seeing Pol—"

"No! Not another word. Go to your bed. Lie down. Stay there till I call you."

Daddy was home early that day. Since Mummy wasn't feeling well, he read me my books as the rain pelted on the tin roof. "Did you see the groundhog today?" he asked.

I shook my head. Always the scientist, he asked, "What other liv-ing things have you seen since we came here?"

"Robins, and blue jays, and a wild canary, and bumble bees, and butterflies, and toads."

"And are all of these real? You're not making them up?"

"No."

"What about Polly? Is she real, or is she just-pretend, like the gin-gerbread man?" He spoke in the voice that I called his teaching voice. Sorry to disappoint him, but I had to tell the truth.

"Polly is real. Here is one of her buttons."

His mouth twitched. "That looks like the buttons on your moth-er's pink sweater. Now, would you like me to read *The Little Engine That Could?*"

Mum felt better the next day, so we drove into town as planned. Going down the lane, I looked back and glimpsed Polly's dress fluttering at the edge of the grove. I was sorry she couldn't accompany us but soon forgot her in the excitement of the ride and the movies on Main Street. After the matinee let out, we went to the grocery, almost deserted at that time of day. As my parents shopped, I kept up a steady stream of chatter. The clerk, stout, white-haired, in a blue smock, smiled at me as I strolled through the store. When we arrived at the check-out, she scrutinized us in friendly fashion.

"You're not from around here, are you?" My parents introduced themselves and explained our reason for being up north. "How nice, to bring the family along! Where are you staying?"

"Out in the country, at the old Clayton place," Mum said. "It's isolated, but we like it. So peaceful."

"A little girl my age lives out there too," I piped up. "Her name is Polly." The clerk blanched. She turned to the youth bagging our groceries. "Take over for me, okay?" She beckoned to my mother and drew her over to two chairs outside the office. "I don't want to spoil your stay here, but what you've said disturbs me," she began. "A tragedy happened at the old Clayton place years ago, when I was a young married woman."

At Mum's elbow, I listened. The clerk had gone to high school with a girl named Flora Clayton, who had grown up in the country on a farm with her parents but boarded in town during the week to get her education. At sixteen, Flora dropped out of school and ran away to the city to work. A few years later, in the depths of the Great Depression, she arrived home with a baby. Her father was angry, but her mother persuaded him to take in Flora and her child.

"I didn't see much of Flora then. She didn't get to town often. Once I saw her and the baby, a pretty little thing called Pauline. Another time, a few years later, I met her in the five-and-dime. She told me she was living with a man in a cabin down the road from her parents' farm. I knew the fellow, a rough sort of guy. He guided for hunters and fishermen. She had rejected his advances before going to the city, but I guess he moved in on her once she was home. She told me her father kicked her out and said never to come back. As we were talking, this fellow came up all tight-lipped, ordered her to quit gabbing, that he was ready to go home. I didn't think much of him, but I didn't know what her life was like until after the fire."

My eyes widened. Polly hadn't mentioned a fire.

The clerk continued her story. Mrs. Clayton, who slipped down every now and then to see Flora and Pauline, or Polly, worried about mysterious bruises on her daughter's and granddaughter's arms and throats. She urged her daughter to leave the man, to come home, throw herself on her father's mercy and ask to be taken in again. Both father and daughter had too much pride to make the first move.

One spring night, a plume of smoke above the trees alerted everyone for miles around. Neighbors followed the smoke and arrived at the site of the cabin to find old Mr. and Mrs. Clayton frantically carrying water in buckets from the creek to throw on the cabin, now flaming to the sky.

The police from town found two bodies in the cabin, not three. The corpses were burned, but knife wounds were still discernable. The fire had been set to hide a double murder. There was no sign of the man. "But Polly didn't die!" I said. "I saw her yesterday. Here's her button."

Three adults stared at me, their mouths hanging open.

That night, Mummy and I left for Toronto by train. The child psychologist I saw soon after did not believe in ghosts, or second sight. The sessions with her were fun, like playing. She soon reported to my mother that I was a normal child who must have overheard some mention of the tragic deaths and made up a story, complete with imaginary friend, as a coping mechanism. I remember overhearing an argument in which Mummy accused Dad not only of setting us up in a house near a horrible crime scene of yesteryear, but also of telling an impressionable child the gory details. Daddy, of course, denied doing so.

The psychologist assured Mummy that I had quite forgotten Polly, and that I chattered freely about my friends, all identifiable, from kindergarten. As for the pearl button, the mental health expert pointed out to Mummy that children were scavengers. I could have found it anywhere.

I never mentioned Polly again. I never saw her anymore. I left her behind on the old Clayton farm, waiting for her grandfather to relent and let her in. Why didn't I see her mother? Perhaps ghosts prefer to appear to people who will be sympathetic to them. I don't think any ghost would appear to Mummy, so down to earth and practical. Maybe several ghosts lived there in the mist, including Polly's grieving grandparents.

Almost half a century has passed since then, and I have seen no other spirits. I wonder if Polly still roams that wilderness farm, making daisy chains and watching the groundhogs. Perhaps the murderer is dead now, and they are all at rest. If not, well, there are worse places to spend eternity.

RUTH LATTA has written four books: *Life Writing*, *The Memory of All That*, *A Wild Streak*, and *Life Music*. She lives in Ottawa with a microbiologist and a cat.

CELEBRATE:
THE 10TH ANNIVERSARY
OF WOMEN'S ORDINATION
TO THE
PRIESTHOOD
SUNDAY JULY 29, 1984
3:00 PM
GRACE EPISCOPAL CHURCH
819 MADISON ST.
SYRACUSE, N.Y.

HR FREEMAN-JONES

Cassandra
in the Temple

ON JULY 29, 1974, ELEVEN OF US WERE ORDAINED as the first women priests in the Episcopal Church. A communion service was part of that event. Full of symbolism. Communion at its simplest is a reenactment of the Last Supper. The meaning of chalice and paten symbolically shown in our tenth-anniversary poster is almost universally understood.

On that July day, in 1974, after over two thousand people had received the bread and wine from women for the first time, an old woman was still kneeling at the altar rail. I thought she might need help getting up and so went to her. She was crying. Through her tears she asked to stay a little longer. She said, "This was the first time I knew it meant me." There is indeed something magical and beautiful when our symbols are commonly understood and when they also reflect reality and *possibility.* Then they unlock ancient mysteries and move us a little closer to a heaven on earth.

But there is another side. In the back of the *Book of Common Prayer* there are "Historical Documents of the Church." Among them are thirty-nine articles of religion established by the bishops, the clergy, and the laity in 1801. These articles are seldom read, even during dull sermons, and, if they were read, they would be mystifying to most. It is impossible, however, to miss the fact that these articles of faith were intended to define the Church of England apart from Rome. The twenty-second article, "Of Purgatory," states: "The Romanish Doctrine concerning Purgatory, Pardons, Worshiping and Adoration, as well as Images as of Relics, and also Invocation of Saints, is a fond thing, vainly invented, and grounded upon no warranty of Scripture, but rather repugnant to the Word of God."

The Church of England was not alone. All branches of the Reformation spent much time and energy getting rid of vestments and other reminders of Rome. In fact there has been trouble (as recorded in holy writ) ever since Moses found the children of Israel worshiping a gold calf, ever since Isaiah complained

> Your countless sacrifices, what are they to me? Says the Lord.
> I am sated with whole-offerings of rams
> and the fat of buffaloes . . .
> New moons and sabbaths and assemblies,
> sacred seasons and ceremonies, I cannot endure.

In a secular setting Isaiah might have been speaking about the Nazis' use of the swastika or the cross-burning by the Ku Klux Klan.

In addition to misuse or use for evil purposes, there is the possibility of misunderstanding. Your symbol may not mean to you what it means to me.

♭ My cousin Keturah, mother's first cousin, was colorful and not at all religious. Over her bed, instead of a pale Jesus, there was a picture of Jefferson Davis draped in the Confederate flag. Born in Kentucky, Keturah lived most of her life in Detroit, where she had invented herself as a woman of Southern grandeur. For years, she served as president of the United Daughters of the Confederacy—this during Detroit's first race riots. For me, this was a "fond thing, vainly invented."

♭ Not too long ago, our daughter, Sarah, living in Wellington, New Zealand, took our three-year-old granddaughter Zoe to a quaint little church in the Wellington suburbs. At the altar, Sarah, thinking it improper for Zoe to receive the bread and wine without understanding what it meant, put her arm across Zoe, who then called out, quite loudly, "What's the matter, mommy, is it too spicy?" bringing home the point that the little girl couldn't yet understand the adults' meaning of the chalice and the paten.

♭ My mother, in her eighties and an ex-Methodist, came with us to our urban Episcopal church where the rector was holding celebration of Rogation Days. The service was held outside and included much praying about the good earth. The good earth we were standing on was hardened mud. Interrupting, mother, who was a little hard of hearing, and may have thought the congregation was praying for better soil, said, "I can see why nothing grows here."

Besides being misunderstood, there are situations in which symbols do not represent the actions they are intended to show. Symbols that do not match action either fade away or actually do harm. Symbols that are private talismans cannot reflect our common humanity or our collective unconscious. On saying this, I now feel like the Cassandra of symbolism. But that is a harsh judgment, too harsh, I think, for I confess to a private love: just before we were ordained, our ordaining bishop, Daniel Corrigan, gave each of us a tiny ceramic pendant that said *Ordain Women.* It had been made by an elderly woman in California. I don't even know her name. Mine has been broken and mended twice. It means more to me than any other churchly artifact because it represents the love and commitment, not of a bishop, nor any other person in power. Many in high places were, and are, against the ordination of women. Rather, my cherished pendant represents "the power of the people" as we used to say in the 1960s. I think God would like that. I think that is what Jesus was about, and there is much biblical warrant for truth being spoken by those considered lowly. When the priest Amaziah complained about the prophet Amos, questioning his credentials, Amos explained that though he was neither a prophet, nor a prophet's son, just a herdsman, and a dresser of sycamore trees, God had chosen him anyway. Young, simple Mary, was chosen as Jesus' mother. Over and over it turns out that it is we, the people, who know and speak the truth. It is our symbols, not the rings of popes and potentates which can make the most sense to us.

The symbolism that lifts my spirit has nothing to do with a church cluttered, as it often is, with meaningless and misinterpreted artifacts. It is instead art that takes us beyond ourselves, art not fixed in time or space or experience, art that moves us to see ourselves and the world we share in new ways.

In the 1950s I found artist Peter Takal. His work was on exhibit at the Everson Museum here in Syracuse. I first bought his *Kneeling Nude.* Little by little I have collected, for me and for our children and grandchildren, other nudes, landscapes, interiors, fish, and plants. Some are etchings, some ink drawings, some lithographs. All are spare. The half-abstract human form, and nature, as beautifully rendered by Takal, allow us to experience beauty, beautifully rendered. Such beauty, Zen-like, moves us beyond that which is private and personal and invites us into a sort of perfection.

This is enough for anyone hoping to make sense of an undigested life.

BETTY BONE SCHIESS lives in Syracuse, New York, where she continues to challenge authority and, among other things, question the value of churchly symbols. As one of the first eleven women ordained as Episcopal priests, she has now collected data to suggest that much Christian iconography is no longer fitting. The Reverend Ms. Schiess has been a member for ten years of the New York State Task Force on Life and the Law, was initiated into the Women's Hall of Fame in 1994, and is listed in *Who's Who in Religion* and in *Who's Who.*

KATHRYN JANE RIPLEY

A Houseful of Guests

Doug Chevalier, 1974.
The Washington Post.
Photograph
of Mr. Kreeger
playing for his wife.

At David Kreeger's
eightieth-birthday
party in 1989,
violinist Isaac Stern
said that Kreeger was
the cultural center
of Washington
long before his home
became one.

ART MUSEUMS can be thought of as treasure houses for symbols where you can see a procession of visual art, the truth of dreams, all compressed into one viewing place. Besides bringing the viewer to its special array of art, Washington's Kreeger Museum itself appears as a procession of airy domes that float behind a high stone wall facing elegant Foxhall Road in the northwest section of the city. The building was designed by twentieth-century architect Philip Johnson as a private dwelling for the Kreeger family as well as a showcase for David Kreeger's extensive art collection and a place to play chamber music. Each museum room dissolves into the next. The architect called his work a Renaissance palace; the contractor referred to it as "the largest three-bedroom house with attached garage in the world." The Renaissance palace and contemporary residence exist comfortably together, bound by art and music.

Although in a churchly or institutional context "dome" may recall the vast and imposing or the remote and reserved, the three saucer domes in the Kreeger Great Hall float in calm light, suspended in informal freedom, quite human in scale. The lunette windows gracing each dome are hung with tiny cork balls strung on teak rods, which convey the charming simplicity of Eastern wooden fretwork shielding interior privacy. Throughout Kreeger's eclectic collection, East meets West in close synergy, and both acknowledge an African heritage. In the entrance hall, an ancient stone *Vishnu* and his two tiny wives gaze inward upon a limestone Mayan head and a third-century Bodisattva. Those images lead outward to Maillol's glorious *Pomona*, autumn goddess and fruitful woman, on the sculpture terrace.

Aristide Maillol. *Pomona. Bronze,* 64½×24½×14⅞ in., 1922. Plaster original made ca. 1907.

As surely as Kreeger's nine Monets are attuned to Debussy, there is a strong and impassioned musical focus throughout the Kreeger collection, from Kandinsky and Leger to Davis and Poons. Gene Davis, Kreeger's friend and also a fine musician, painted *Untitled* with dazzling rhythms and rich harmonies marking a change from Davis's familar use of deep, saturated hues to the lighter, semi-pastels of his late works. Larry Poons, himself a graduate of the New England Conservatory of Music, created a shimmering painting that hangs in the Contemporary Gallery and is alive with small dancing shapes. In fact, music is the subtle element that weaves the tangible and ethereal into one sublime union in this museum. As a tribute to Kreeger, after his death in 1990, the Ying Quartet joined by the St. Lawrence Quartet played the Kreeger favorite, Mendelssohn's

Gene Davis. *Untitled.* Acrylic on canvas, 68×68 in., 1969.

Octet, in the museum's great hall. The memory of baroque and ancient harmonies blends with contemporary polyphonies there. Those Byzantine domes also reflect human sounds and actually resonate with past murmurs and whispers in unexpected niches. Guests are astonished when two of them speak softly in a small space beside the Picasso *Café de La Rotonde,* only to discover that a third person, standing in a niche beside Chagall's

Pablo Picasso. *Café de La Rotonde.* Oil on canvas, 18×32 in., 1901.

Marc Chagall.
Composition. 1912.
Oil on canvas, 27×22 in.

Composition hanging diagonally across the wide Great Hall, can hear their whispered words.

The Kreeger Museum collection, like any collection, and the building in which it is housed offer an opportunity to see transcendent truth by going through ordinary objects as the eye seizes upon an image and the mind discovers an inner world. In Miro's *Deux Personnages, for example,* a rope, some nails, an Altamira Cave figure, and blood-red fangs give an insight into Spain under the agony of Franco and the approach of the Spanish Civil War. Color particularly evokes emotion, embellishes dreams, and engulfs the soul. "The bluebird of happiness," "the black night of despair," and "the red badge of courage" may be clichés, but they are instantly recognizable. Our atavistic response to pure color is enhanced by light and texture, and from this magical union, color emerges as a powerful spirit that can help us understand meaning.

Through a landscape or a still life or an abstract sculpture, there is an illumination of the truth of dreams or fairy tales or history. Monet's dreamlike landscape of his beloved Pourville Cliffs uses bro-

Claude Monet.
Impression du coucher de soleil, Falaises de Pourville.
[Impression of sunset, Cliffs at Pourville].
Oil on canvas
23⅝×32⅛ in., 1882.

ken color and broken brush strokes to heighten the emotional impact of two solitary figures bathed in thin, light air in a vast expanse of sea and sky and sand. As in visions and dreams, nothing is clear-cut and solid in the work of Monet or the Impressionists in general. Nature is veiled in atmosphere; objects are seen as vibrations or sensations of light and color, rather than shapes and forms.

Strange tales can be spun around Picasso's 1914 *Still Life,* where a newspaper torn to shreds lies beside a glass, and a dagger is half concealed with its blade wrenched from the hilt and all the surface is sprinkled with sand and bound with rope. Though these flat and colored shapes are arranged decoratively on the canvas, the scene evokes a haunting, tortured, nightmare image.

Fernand Leger, the modernist painter of steel and concrete industrial forms, uses the familiar geometry of the factory to present *Child with Accordion.* The soft, rounded outlines of the child contrast with the cool line of the steel beam he sits upon. Strange clouds float behind him in the orange sky. We strain to hear the music as this realistic little fellow pumps his accordion in a hymn to life and a symbol of hope.

On the sculpture terrace Henry Moore's *Reclining Figure—Bridge Prop* invites a spirited dialogue. The three separate, rounded volumes of this female figure, each with a quietly textured surface, blend into their feminine inspiration: The Waterloo Bridge, symbol and reality expressed in abstract monumental bronze. Lucien Wercollier's astonishing abstract bronze sculpture *Formes Spatiales* with its black patina, placed in one of the museum gardens, teases the imagination. Its negative spaces are entirely equal to the positive. The eye explores the open interior and is drawn outward. Forms in space, as well as spacial forms appear to float mysteriously without a base.

Henry Moore. *Three-piece Reclining Figure No. 2: Bridge-prop.* Bronze, 41½×98³/8×44½ in., 1963.

In the three great Vanitas works of Georges Braque, a sense of mourning is evoked by the encompassing stillness of the composition and an ambiguous spacial structure, unusual in Braques' work. In muted colors, with the absence of strong action lines, the prominence of a skull affirms a Vanitas work. Braque's use of a melancholy palette prompts emotion; lavender hues recall death, grief, and loss. Specifically, in the small *Vanitas 1,* there are displayed, along with the skull, a crucifix and a Rosary, all strong testaments to sorrow and prayer and the fragility of human existence. Vanitas' symbols encompass time and space. In American art of the nineteenth century, Vanitas' works were known as Momenti Mori. An 1815 masterpiece by Charles Byrd King, *Poor Artist's Cupboard,* has as its central symbol a skull and evidence of deteriorating senses abounds.

Camille Pissarro. *Le Jardin des Tuileries.* Oil on canvas, 21½×35¾, 1900.

Mondrian's fantastic *Dying Sunflower,* strangely beautiful and confounding in its conflated image, commands attention to negative connotations: aging, illness, and death, as well as positive parallel aspects of maturity and grace. The muted yellow and gold are deeper and richer than the brilliant yellow of youth. In all living organisms, the process is inescapable, beautiful and unapologetic in elegant decay.

Piet Mondrian.
Dying Sunflower.
Water color on paper,
37½×14½ in.,
1907–1908.

A late work by de Stael, *Flowers in a Red Vase,* conveys a similar message. While not a Vanitas work, it seems to presage the artist's suicide. He uses the same blood-red pigment as did Oscar Blummer in his last sad paintings, which were also a portent of his suicide. In addition, de Stael's transference of the white roses to black foreshadows sorrow and confusion. Not all aging is reserved to twilight shadows, sorrow, and confusion. *Les Jardins des Tuillerird,* painted by Pissarro in his last years is so dazzling in its springtime greens and mottled sunlight, with what might be Debussy's *Engulfed Cathedral* shimmering in the background, that youth seems to be its creator.

Alongside these works is a mix of art and artifacts collected half a century ago in Africa. Although never created for museum display, this folk art engages the most sophisticated mind with its simplicity and clarity. On a fertility mask from the Baga people of New Guinea, the mystery of its scarification defies interpretation. The complex ideology of the Naiu people weaves a fanciful myth of man, animal, water, and savannah around a crocodile mask indicating the unity of all things. A circle of images embraced in a primitive wooden mask illuminates the inward seeking after meaning and designates universal truth.

To move from the sometimes portentous symbols of aboriginal tribes to the serenity of the sculpture terrace in the Kreeger museum may be something of a culture shock, as Henry Moore and Jacques Lipchitz demand attention. The eye is captivated by the sensuous curves of Arp's bronzes, while the heart opens to Nagouchi's *Soliloquy.* Standing in isolated loneliness, it portrays the human condition, drawing from the collective unconscious, and turning to the mysteries of the creative process.

In a setting of protective grandeur amidst ancient trees and the alluring scent of distant blossoms, the stillness of the moment becomes the essence of experience. In the words of Odilon Redon whose works grace the collection, "the quest for meaning is the slow and gradual process of seeking synthesis between the certain and the uncertain, between physics and metaphysics." The constant might of image can instruct, illumine, and inspire. A procession through any museum is a journey of spiritual discovery. In the Kreeger, ordinary and specific references of art and architecture, setting and sound, reveal truths beyond time and place.

KATE RIPLEY is coordinator of the docents at the Kreeger Museum in Washington, D.C. (which can be visited by appointment only). She was previously editor of *The Journal of Community and Junior Colleges.*

W. JOE INNIS

The House That George Haunts

ALREADY HE'S STARTED—MY WORTHY ANCESTOR, a painter like myself. You'd think he'd stay in the studio where he can complain about my brushwork, but no, he's a critic of my writing as well. Doesn't like my opening. Lacks dignity, he says. Fine.

He's bent at the waist, looking over my shoulder at the screen in front of us. He snorts in derision, points a bony finger to the part where I call him George.

I lie a little, tell him I'll fix it later. He offers other suggestions, and I pretend to greet them with the same gravity I give to his ideas on painting. But he's a terrible writer. I don't know whether he knows that, and I see no need to tell him. He can be prickly. Always was, as I understand it. Though I've known him only recently, I gather from the biography his son George Jr. wrote that the artist was a tad testy, though you had to read between the lines. The trashing of parents wasn't yet fashionable when the book was penned.

This house that George Inness (1825–1894) haunts is just up the Hudson from his birthplace in Newburgh. I've taken it on lease, mainly because it's similar to the one in Milton a few miles to the north where he painted when he wanted to get out of Montclair and New Jersey. That was during the last, and by far the most fruitful, decade of his life. Three-story Victorians we call them now. Though a lot of new stuff has been built between us, the west bank hasn't changed much since the mid-1880s. Still rolling farms with plenty of Italy to go around. Apple trees march over undulating land, breaking ranks for a weathered barn; velvet skies drape over fields of spring grass. Though Octobers bring less in the way of leaf burnings than in Inness's day, the clouds are still Constable's.

George Inness. *Wood Gatherers: An Autumn Afternoon.* Oil on canvas, 30×45¹/₈ in., 1891. Sterling and Francine Clark Art Institute, Williamstown, Massachusetts.

Inness was painting over his head when he lived here, which is to say he was painting as an artist, beyond himself and his early workmanlike, if entirely competent, efforts. By then he'd been declared the leading American landscape painter of his time. If that was excessive, it wasn't by far. Whether it was his passion for the vision of Swedenborg or because he was just damn good, he painted then like no one else, this bearded old man who stands in the dark just behind me.

He was said to bridle at those who would link him to the Impressionists, a club he despised, partly, I suppose, because they wouldn't have him when he could have used their notoriety, and partly because he didn't think they could paint. Nor was he fond of being included in the Hudson River School. Here he was on stronger ground. His paintings were far too intimate and not nearly geographical enough for that tradition. A Jasper Cropsey, Sanford Gifford, or Frederick Church, his immediate contemporaries, he was not. The long and precise view didn't interest him as did symbolism. When he was pressed to conform to the standards of a commission, it showed.

Even his painting, *Niagara,* couldn't be accused of anything but what it was, the muted crash of water as seen through a veil of mist lit like a cache of emeralds in the sun. Among the many liberties he

Photograph of George Inness, 1889. Photographs of Artists— Collection I. Archives of American Art, Smithsonian Institution, Washington, D.C.

took was his hawk's-eye view of the falls, suspending the view just over them. This, at the time when spectators had to know exactly where they stood.

No, he was closer to the younger James McNeill Whistler, who spent some unhappy years nearly getting himself tossed out of West Point. Much later, his self-imposed exile alternating between Paris and his place on the Thames, Whistler would learn to make weather out of his soup of subtle glazes, beating Inness chronologically to the tonal glow that eventually would dominate the work of both.

(All right, George. I hear you. But I didn't use the word "steal." Didn't even imply it. Although you must admit, all of us crib a little, lean on history, our contemporaries. Don't tell me you weren't taken by the way Corot could feather the leaves of his trees into the damp of the sky behind them. Who wasn't? Or how Millet rooted his figures to the earth. Not you? You didn't borrow—just a little—from Turner, Monet, Renoir, Boudin, Poussin and Jongkind? Okay, you did Europe with your eyes closed. I'm talking about the rest of us.)

In addition to a striking resemblance to a portrait of my great grandfather and the sound of Scotland in our last names—Inness is said to have fancied his up some—we also share pretty much the same view of the river from our second floor studios, a love for skies and trees and how they reflect themselves in the streams and ponds around, and the way clouds in this part of the world can ignite them. And how greens behave when they're set against a warm wash of sienna; the way an ochre cloud swells and scuttles over the flat blue beneath it. This is the language we use when he isn't breathing over my shoulder, telling me how to write.

I doubt it's news to those who live as artists—today or any other—that we take counsel from those who walked the earth before us. Most of us who paint do so for those not yet born. We're not comfortable with the world we inhabit. Often we find solace in our churches, the museums that harbor our gods. You've seen us, if you'd bothered to notice, standing within inches of a painting on the wall, drinking in color, the sweep of a brush, leaning towards it, as though listening for something. Our shabby clothes should not be seen as a fashion statement.

We're alone mostly, so maybe you can understand how we can be open to mystical suggestion, hear and feel things others don't, won't. In choosing our friends it doesn't seem right to exclude those we talk to most. That they're dead is only a temporal impediment.

I'm prodded now, a touch on the shoulder, a stirring of the air. It's hard to say how he does this. He wants me to remind you that we're talking about artists before the word got cheapened, before it became an excuse for doing anything at all, and I see his point. A distinction should be made.

The artists George and I have in mind have shunned fashion, as did Inness himself most of his life. They believe in understanding the visual tools and social context they inherit and using them to tell a truth larger than the life it comes from, a contemporary truth. They craft their work in paint, clay, and granite and find these materials no more limiting than words to a novelist.

And you'll come to find in the work these artists do, at least a little of the dynamics contained in so many of the late Inness paintings, most importantly, the uplifting sense of life that comes when the spirit is moved.

Sorry. I'll get back to you. He's out in the studio again, rummaging through my stack of canvases, talking to himself. Grumbling, the way he does.

W. JOE INNIS is an international painter with solo shows in major capitals, including Tokyo, Seoul, Buenos Aires, Istanbul, and New York. *Also Rising*, his second novel and third book, was published in January. His relationship to George Inness is less biological than spiritual. A painting by Joe Innis illustrated "The Way of Flowers" in this issue.

MICHAEL ROBARTES

Lawn Doctor

YUN WAS NEARLY FINISHED AND WAS GLAD. He did not like working for the doctor.

To Yun, Doctor Feingold was everything that was wrong with the world. Yun was a gardener—a good one—and he knew it was the doctors of the world who were at the heart of the confusion. He often wished that he could go back home to his native land.

For the doctor, it was completely different. He knew how Yun felt. Doctor Feingold understood that it was just the Chinaman's way of dealing with the civilized world. He knew that Yun, while not a wealthy man, was basically a good one. The only problem the doctor had was that sometimes the gardener wanted a little too much money for his services.

On this day, it took Yun just under three hours to complete his work. He manicured everything to perfection. He cut back the ivy to the edge of the bed, so that it did not cascade over the concrete border, unkempt and scraggly. Then he cut the lawn with the outlandish and noisy mower he carried on the back of his small pickup truck. Yun stopped to admire its clipped uniformity. He bent to one knee

Ogata Korin. Six-panel Japanese screen (one of a pair): *Iris and Bridge*. Paint on paper, 70½×146¼ in., Seventeenth to eighteenth century. The Metropolitan Museum of Art, Purchase, Louisa Eldridge McBurney Gift, 1953 (53.7.2).

and rubbed his hand across the newly-cut lawn, much as he tousled the closely-cropped hair of his five-year-old grandson. He took his rake and evened out the sand that surrounded the stone bench that lay beneath the two Monterey Pines in the back yard. Artfully, he shaped the evenly-rounded markings of the rake, as in a Zen monastery. He liked the way that particular corner of the doctor's garden looked as it oversaw the ocean below. He wondered if the doctor's wife ever came out here with her coffee to breathe the fresh sea air.

Yun walked slowly to the front door. This was the moment he dreaded. Now he had to try and pry a few pennies away from the doctor. The doctor was so close-fisted with his money, and yet he had so much. Yun shook his head and looked sadly at the large white house before him with the curving blacktop driveway, shaded by graceful maple trees that swayed a bit in the breeze. He thought of the swimming pool in the backyard, its water a pure and innocent blue, and of the two cream-colored automobiles that sat in the garage.

A sigh escaped him.

Yun was glad the work was done. Everything always took so long here, and if he was not careful, his back would start to ache. And now that he was finished with the work, he was faced with the unpleasant task of convincing the doctor that it was honorable to pay Yun what was due.

He paused a moment before the front door. He could hear music coming from inside. The doctor was listening to a recorded opera, probably sitting in the soft leather chair Yun had seen through the patio doors. Yun could picture the man there, erect and attentive, forming opinions of authority. Yun prepared himself for battle. Somehow, the doctor thought himself a great and generous man.

Yun rang the bell. In a few moments the doctor was there. He smiled brightly, confidently. "How much do I owe you, Yun?"

Yun stood up straight. He was a head shorter than the doctor. He focused all his thought on his voice. It took a great effort to speak to the doctor. "It is thirty dollars, sir," he said, looking him directly in the eye. It was all he could do to get the words out.

The doctor shook his head. He was chewing a small bit of food absent-mindedly. "No," he said, shaking his head and picking at his teeth with his tongue. Then he smiled confidently. "No, Yun, that is too much. It is not yet three full hours. Twenty-five dollars will be fine." He reached into his back pocket for his wallet, which was thick with identification, bills, and credit cards, and made of a smooth brown leather. "I will give you twenty-five."

Yun was wounded mortally. It was like this every time. He did not know what to say, he was so very sad. It had been but five minutes short of three hours, and he had worked enthusiastically, without stopping.

Again he summoned all his courage. "It is much closer to three hours than two and a half, sir." It was all he could do to control himself, and still his voice had changed to a bit of a whine.

The doctor did not like the sound of it. "No, Yun, that is not the way things are done. You have not been here three hours, and you certainly took a break. The lawn looks very fine, as always, but" and here he looked significantly at the smaller man, "the world is full of gardeners, Yun." He looked deeply into Yun's eyes. "Please take twenty-five dollars from my hand. It will be enough."

Yun bowed slightly, and took the money. It was always like this. As he turned away, his eyes went to the heavens. On the way down the steps he said a small prayer in Chinese. He thanked the Goddess for sending the doctor to him. Smiling to himself, the little gardener praised Kwan Yin for teaching him about plants and the way things grow, full of the knowledge that given three hours he could make anyone's garden look like a million dollars.

MICHAEL ROBARTES is a California writer, who has recently written the libretto to an opera by Paul Hurley entitled *Georg Schaeffer Loves Adolph Hitler*. He has also completed a film script on the life of Tchaikovsky, *A Divine Madness*.

Chinese Wedding

Paul and Eng-Li were married in the Year of the Dragon, the most charismatic of the twelve animals in the Chinese astrological cycle. The pen-and-ink drawing is by Rebecca Kingery, 1989.

SWIRLING AROUND THE SURFACE OF THE SWEET SOUP, the dried flower is deftly plucked with our shared china spoon and offered to me. In Cantonese, the flower is called *pak hup*. The sound of its name is similar to a phrase that means 'a hundred years together', so appropriate as we sit here on my future-wife's bed on our wedding day.

Eng-Li and I met in Kuala Lumpur, Malaysia, on my second day in the country. I had arrived to take up a lectureship at the University of Malaya where Eng-Li was a graduate student. Three years later, at the end of my contract, we married. The year was 1988, Year of the Dragon, the most charismatic of the twelve animals in the Chinese astrological cycle. The dragon symbolizes spirit and therefore commands respect; it is also regarded as a "lucky" creature. Thus, the Year of the Dragon, usually sees an increase in weddings and births amongst the Chinese. The year 1988 is also significant because the sound of the number eight, or *baat,* is similar to the sound of the word for prosperity, or *faat.* Because the Chinese language is tonal in nature, similarity of sounds forms the basis of many symbolic traditions.

Eng-Li is third-generation Chinese Malaysian on her father's side, while her mother is Chinese Vietnamese. Generally, modern Malaysians no longer observe many of the traditional wedding rituals, but we decided to incorporate some of the more important ones into our wedding.

For Eng-Li, the first ritual is the hair-combing ceremony performed in her home by her mother the night before the wedding day. According to custom, I should have been going through the same ceremony with my mother, at the exact same moment. However, I was far from my home in England, and my mother was unable to fly out for our wedding. In this ceremony the hair is ritually combed to symbolize the attainment of maturity. While drawing a comb through the bride's hair, her mother proclaims her to be a woman and repeats blessings for her future married life.

On the day of the wedding, I set out shortly after dawn with a posse of male friends or *tang chiun sek* (literally, "ram through stone") in a Mercedes tastefully festooned with red ribbons and rosettes. From my house at Taman Seputih on the outskirts of the city, we head across Petaling Jaya and to my future wife's house in Taman Tun Dr. Ismail with the intent of breaching the bride's fortress.

At Eng-Li's house I am helped out of my carriage by Eng-Li's youngest brother, and in exchange I present him a *hoong pow* or "red packet" containing a token sum of money. To the Chinese, red is an auspicious color, and a red packet of money is a traditional way of giving. We are confronted with a locked security grid behind which is a group of young women, friends, and family of Eng-Li. Somehow we have to gain entry. Negotiation is the key. In days past, this may have involved some bartering over the balance of the bride-price, but in these modern times the men are usually asked to perform a number of tasks. Beneath the entrance way, which is draped with a nine-foot-nine-inches long red cloth with the words "nine" and "long" repeated twice, meaning long lasting or enduring, we show off our singing talent. After proving my ability to declare "I love you" in ten languages, we make numerous declarations of sincerity. Having satisfied the women guards, we are finally allowed in.

My first sight of the sweet soup follows our successful entry of the female household. Eng-Li's mother is there, holding the soup bowl. With her hands on one side and mine on the other, she wishes us a long and happy married life. Eng-Li is secreted in her chamber upstairs with her friends. Bearing a bridal bouquet of red orchids and the bowl of sweet soup, I lead my group upstairs to the barred door of the bridal chamber, where again we negotiate with the women for entry to the chamber.

After entering the chamber and presenting a bouquet to Eng-Li, we sit on the bed sharing the soup. The *pak hup* flowers are not the only things in the soup. There are little *tang yuin,* sweet, sticky, round dumplings made of glutinous rice flour to represent sweet proximity and togetherness in marriage; and red dates or *hoong choe* signifying early success; and lotus seeds, *lin chee,* the continuation of generations. The sounds of these words are similar to the sounds of the words for their symbolic meanings. The sweetness of the soup symbolizes the hope for good times together. We share the soup, each in turn offering the other some tasty and significant morsel, and finish it to the very last drop, symbolizing that we will stay together to the end.

After eating the soup, I lead Eng-Li down the stairs to the main room of the house where, seated in a simple wooden chair, Eng-Li's hundred-year-old grandfather awaits the tea ceremony. We kneel on the floor, face him, and I nervously offer him Chinese tea in a Chinese tea-cup. If he accepts the tea and takes even one sip, he is accepting me as a suitable groom. To my relief, he drinks the tea, replacing the tea-cup on the tray along with a *hoong pow.* Then we offer tea to all of the family, serving the oldest first. When we reach those family members younger than ourselves, it is they who offer tea to us. During the ceremony, Eng-Li's mother gives her a *hoong pow* of gold as does her sister, adorning her with gold necklaces and bracelets.

For the ceremonies that take place during the day, I dress in an off-white linen suit; but because white is a color of mourning, I wear a red tie and red orchid in my lapel. Eng-Li opts for a violet silk dress with red orchids in her hair.

Traditionally, there should be a reciprocal ritual at my house in which Eng-Li is accepted by my family. In times past, this would have been the more important because the bride married "into" the groom's family and went to live with her husband and his family. This second tea ceremony formalizes the marriage.

With the ceremonies at Eng-Li's home completed, I lead her to the car. She is escorted by her grandfather who holds an umbrella over her while her mother showers her with rice, symbolizing their hope that Eng-Li will be well provided with food and shelter in her new life. Eng-Li's mother also gives her a basket containing the comb that was used in the hair-combing ceremony, and the tea set used in the tea ceremony, as well as two bowls, two pairs of chopsticks with a small packet of rice, two *hoong pows,* and two silk dressing gowns—

all symbols of her hope that we will have a happy marriage, blessed with good fortune and plenty.

In the old days, the bride would also be accompanied by her bridal trousseau and furnishings for the bridal chamber, and a band of musicians would herald the party's progress to the groom's house. We do not have the musicians, but we are escorted by a convoy of our friends in cars decked with red ribbons and balloons.

Back at my house, I refrain from aiming a well-planted kick at the car door before helping Eng-Li out of the bridal carriage. Traditionally this kick symbolized the authority that the groom would assume over his bride. Instead, I observe the Western custom of carrying Eng-Li over the threshold under another nine-foot-nine-inches long red cloth draped over my door. Once inside the house we repeat the tea ceremony by offering tea to my brother, the sole representative of my family in Malaysia. He drinks and offers a *hoong pow* in return, accepting Eng-Li into the Green family.

East meets West after the second tea ceremony when we celebrate at midday with French champagne. Before retiring for an afternoon of rest to prepare us for the evening banquet, there is yet another tradition to be satisfied. I am younger than my brother, and he is unmarried. Younger siblings should wait their turn for marriage. If a younger sibling ties the knot first, on the wedding day the sibling should exit the house wearing a pair of the older sibling's trousers as a sign of respect. This has been slightly modified in some Chinese families to the presenting of an item of clothing by the younger sibling to the older. I give my brother a Malay sarong, a long length of cloth sewn up into a tube, and worn tied around the waist like a skirt.

The wedding banquet is held in our favorite Chinese restaurant. I dress for this in a dark blue suit and, as blue is also a mourning color, I offset it once again with a red bow tie and a red carnation in my lapel. Eng-Li wears a loose *cheong sam*, a traditional Chinese gown of brightly colored silk rich in red and green hues, with red carnations in her hair. Our wedding banquet is a fairly modest affair of ten round tables, each seating ten guests, a good even number. The Chinese avoid seating guests in odd numbers, and round tables are preferred, since the smooth round shape represents wholeness and harmony. We arrive early with family members to receive our guests who do not give wedding gifts but follow the Chinese custom of presenting a *hoong pow* containing an even sum of money, generally in an even number of new bills.

The banquet consists of eight courses starting with a platter of four different appetizers representing the four seasons. This is followed by a golden, crispy roast chicken dish, shark's fin soup with only a symbolic dusting of shark's fin, stir-fried vegetables with assorted mushrooms, a whole steamed fish, tiger prawns in a spicy sauce, fried rice, and a dessert of steamed buns with a sweet lotus seed paste filling (to accompany a sweet longan, literally, "dragon's eyes"), and lotus seed soup. The traditional banquet includes roast suckling pig, but in deference to our Muslim friends, this was dropped from the menu, and we had prawns instead. Fish is an important item on any celebratory menu as the phrase "to have fish" also sounds like "to have a surplus" or "to have more." Chicken is also a must, being a stand-in for the phoenix, which is the female equivalent of the dragon, while shark's fin is a dish for longevity and for royalty.

In a traditional banquet, speeches are made at the beginning before the food is served. However, our best man, being English, makes his speech Western-style halfway through the feasting. Chinese custom is observed when the newly-wedded couple pass from table to table to be toasted by the guests. At each table, we lift our glasses three times with everyone raising voices each time in a drawn-out chorus of "Ya . . a . . a . . m Seng." Literally, this means "bottoms up," but it also sounds like "drink to success." The toasting becomes a competitive event, with each table vying to make their *Yam Seng* louder and longer than the previous table's. By the time we reach the last table, the hall resounds with our guests' good wishes for our success.

Chinese dinners end as soon as the last course is finished: guests usually do not linger but get up and leave, as any festivities are meant to take place during the meal itself. In our case, we leave the banquet hall as soon as the feast ends, but a large party adjourns to our house to continue the celebration into the early hours.

PAUL GREEN grew up in Cambridge, England, and for more than twenty years has been professionally involved with birds. Currently he works for the American Birding Association in Colorado. ENG-LI GREEN grew up in Port Dickson, Malaysia, and, although trained as a zoologist, now runs a desktop publishing company in Great Britain.

PART III

Roses Unfolding

Complete in the Moment

THERE IS NO GUARANTEE OF A SECOND CHANCE
to see through any particular symbol,
whether the symbol is a thing, a person, a relationship,
or an evanescent alignment of circumstances.

Seeing through a symbol
calls for an unprejudiced openness,
what Coleridge descibed as
a willing suspension of disbelief.
Sometimes this receptivity
results from focus or expectation
(as when visiting the crumbling walls,
the ancient ruins that Wordsworth loved,
or following the principles and ritual
of formal flower arranging),
sometimes from crisis, intensity of grief or longing
(as when memory and expectation intersect for a father
or when the drive to *do* and the courage to *be*
collide in a young girl).

—ROBERT H. KIRVEN

ARLENE DISTLER

Nautilus

It arrived in the mail without fanfare,
its cover the bleached tan
of tropical sand, stucco, sun;
a chambered shell drawn
on its front: species "Common Paper"
guidebooks say washes up at times
on Florida shores . . .
a relic from junior high my parents
must've unearthed from some closet corner.

Inside, rows of stamp-size photos
take me by surprise, by lack of it,
these faces, decades later,
engraved on my mind . . .
Even ones I called foolish
or fast, or whose beauty stunned;
those who I shunned, or they me,
for envy . . . their names reverberate—
Emily, Roberta, Howard . . .
Abby, whose gentleness was like shade
to those heated, awkward days;
Bill, whose surname
named his failed organ,
made of him mystery of the given,
the taken away.

And those who cried for the rest of us,
blessed in their want of guile.
Each one is present in full dimension,
imbued with their own tone and hue;
each is as a lover lost
and I pine for them as a lover would,
this sweet ache like the pearl cord
of secreted spine
the mollusk leaves behind
as it moves to its next perimeter
in its spiral crescent climb.

ARLENE DISTLER lives in Brattleboro, Vermont, with her husband and their blended family of five children. She currently spends her time as a producer and videographer for local-access cable TV and is working on a chapbook manuscript.

DUANE TUCKER

Flowers

for Dad's Birthday

What if everything we know was inside out & the sea was
a mud & shell-shelled mountain & mountains were plunging
brown lakes? What if what we see is only what we think

& what we think is but a cloud around the skin of things?
Or if heaven is a basket dangling batlike
below the opalescent orb of creation & hell floats above

the clouds? We could be creatures of the underworld:
tubers & microbes & beetles humusing air-soil,
as we tunnel beneath the blossom of life.

Perhaps trees actually grow down & gravity pulls up & keeps
us bobbing on an endless sea of amniotic air, feeling
the kicks of new life as earthquake & eruption; wind-cry

& hail-ping as infant plea for nourishment?
Or that dark tangle we think
are roots is actually forests of flowers; & strolling

through them, etched against the sun-squandered haze
of loam, we can finally see: each atom as ember,
& embers burning within embers, everything

curtained with fluffy seeds of light, drifting like noon
rain up from earth's womb, through soil-skin,
grass-pore, orifice of shifted stone, seeping

then, into our flesh, filling the bones
with a sort of fire that heals whatever
we touch with petal-wings of indigo & gold.

DUANE TUCKER is a film and TV actor, a screenwriter and poet, whose poetry has
been published widely and has won several awards. His screenplay on John
Muir was recently optioned for production, and he is currently performing in
a one-man play on Muir throughout the U.S.

JAN SHOEMAKER

Tintern Abby

Jervis McEntee.
The Ruins of Caesar's Palace. Oil on canvas,
24¼×40⅛ in.,
ca. 1868.
The Pennsylvania
Academy of the Fine
Arts, Philadelphia. Funds
provided by the Fine
Arts Ball
and Discotheque,
the Pennsylvania
Academy Women's
Committee.

THIS IS A PILGRIMAGE, TO BE SURE. The ruined cathedral toward which we have pointed our rented car is my saint's bit of bone and, in my desire to approach it, I better understand those pilgrims driven to cross the desert to Mecca, the hundred-mile hikers to Santiago, the jet-lagged faithful kneeling before the wailing wall. And as we wind warily along the left side of this narrow road toward Wales, its hairpin turns nowhere evident on the map, I feel a kinship for those other pilgrims who, in a secular world, still seek a holy land.

My husband, white-knuckled behind the wheel, has indulged my desire, keenly felt, to visit this decrepit abbey built by Cistercians in the twelfth century, closed by Henry VIII during the monastic Dissolution four-hundred years later, and made famous by Wordsworth nearly two centuries ago. For years I have guided my students through Wordsworth's *Tintern Abbey* and as I've breathed in its rhythms and pronounced its words, forcing the pitch of my voice to rise and fall with cadences I hope will impart the power of the poem, it has made its home inside me. This first trip into the deep valley of the River Wye is, then, a homecoming.

We are proceeding west along the A40 from Gloucester, a mid-size town in the English Cotswolds, a region of soft slopes that reaches almost to the Welsh border. The ease we enjoyed motoring along the "dual carriageway" (leave it to the English to make even an expressway sound quaint) abated when our four comfortable lanes narrowed to two and the stone walls, so picturesque on postcards, encroached nearly onto the road to form its indisputable boundaries. They speak to me of scratched paint and rending flesh in the universal language of jagged rock as we whiz past them in our sporty Peugot. I shift onto my right thigh, hang awkwardly over the stick shift embedded in my husband's left hand, try futilely to occupy some safer middle seat the car does not provide, and fall back against the door as we pointedly veer left at every roundabout. (These roundabouts, rotaries in America, replace stoplights in most small towns and it takes a peculiar assertiveness, concentration, and agility to maneuver them. More than once, when we first began driving in Britain, we edged into the outer lane too quickly and shot onto an unknown road in the wrong direction.) But today we prevail and in the light rain maintain our course past fields of imperturbable sheep toward Wales.

We are following signs to Ross-on-Wye, *sylvan Wye,* I say out loud, but my husband, preoccupied with keeping to the left, doesn't inquire after poetry and, reaching Ross, we turn south and cross into Wales. Just over the border, and Wales looks wilder than England. Its steeper slopes are thickly forested, and a mist hangs over the hills. At Monmouth we turn onto the A466. "Tintern Ten" promises a marker tucked into the high hedges that line the road. We proceed south; the Wye is off to our right now, moving slowly through its deep ravine, and the damp mid-morning light becomes a green glow as the 466 enters a long stand of trees that close in a canopy over our heads. Road parallels river here along the banks that Wordsworth hiked "a few miles above Tintern Abbey." This, then, is the place— these the "steep and lofty cliffs," the "groves and copses." We drink it in greedily and press on to the abbey, determined to have it all.

"Weak Bridge" we read, pausing for a red light at a one-lane bridge; we cross it on the green. The Wye runs along to our left now, and we follow it into Tintern, a village that lines up along its one main street. The tall, stone facades of houses and shops are shuttered and silent on this late Sunday morning; the single pub is open for business, but the proprietor's wife is in bed with a cold, so there'll be no tea and, for us at least, it's still too early for beer. This, our first

Welshman, is sorry, of course, but not to despair, there is a pub near the abbey, and he points us down the road.

Tintern Abbey rises austere and magnificent against the brooding Welsh sky. Neither the highway that runs directly past it nor the small commerce that cozies up along one side (a souvenir stall, a tea shop, the promised pub) undermine the grandeur of these Gothic arches that hold the sky. We seek refuge from what is clearly a resolute drizzle ("perhaps it will blow over") inside "The Anchor" pub and tearoom; *anchor of my purest thoughts,* I recite, well pleased that if we must encounter tourism it at least inclines to the literary.

My husband, an American history teacher, misses the allusion and disappears through an unmarked doorway. It is into a confusion of color and noise and the smell of wet wool that I follow him. Card tables covered with old books, chipped cups, and costume jewelry clutter a room crowded with locals in damp coats who jostle each other good naturedly, fingering the merchandise. We have stumbled onto a "jumble" sale here at the solemn feet of towering Tintern Abbey—monument to the lofty aspirations of Church and Letters. It is a spectacle likely to offend a literary or ecclesiastical purist, but with no such pretensions (or apologies) we shoulder our way through the crowd and emerge half an hour later triumphant and possessed of a well-used black umbrella for which we gladly paid three pounds.

It costs two pounds twenty to enter "Abaty Tyndyrn" (in Welsh), payable in the gift shop adjacent to the Abbey. Inside Tintern Abbey we are grateful for the extra umbrella as we wander across its sequestered central lawn and along its roofless corridors. Moss softens these stern monastic walls and small ferns sprout from cracks between its rough, weathered stones. These stones, we are informed by discreetly placed plaques, still stand where they were dragged, lifted, and set by monks eight hundred years ago in the service of Spirit, in the pursuit of order. The Cistercians were agriculturalists, we learn, who deliberately chose such remote areas in which to build their abbeys. Tintern Abbey, the first Cistercian house in Wales, prospered into the fourteenth century when, like other medieval institutions, it suffered a social and economic decline as a consequence of plague. Its end as a farming community, as a house of worship, was secured in the 1530s when Henry VIII severed ties with Rome and ordered the suppression of all religious houses. On September 3, l536, the Abbey was seized and sacked by the king's men. Abandoned, it fell into ruin.

Tintern Abbey already enjoyed a modest tourism when Wordsworth visited it in 1798. Cleared by that time (by order of the fifth duke of Beaufort) of the vines and brambles that had overrun it, this ruined monastery could not have looked so different to Wordsworth than it appears to us today. Its double row of Gothic arches lined the same grassy courtyard. The same monolithic arch, designed in the Middle Ages to admit celestial light, dominated its presbytery. Its huge, paneless window overlooked the same stretch of the River Wye, framing the forested hills that rise suddenly from the far bank. In these hills Wordsworth *felt a presence that disturbed* [him] *with the joy of elevated thought.*

I resist the urge to try to imagine myself of such a *presence*, not really believing another person's revelation can be borrowed, shared, or recreated. The *spirit that impels all thinking things* is, I have long believed, universal and makes itself known each moment we stop to listen for it. If it inhabits this place at all, it accompanies and departs with each visitor. Why, then, the difficult drive? Why my compulsion to occupy this ruin, even briefly, to run my hands over its uneven stone? It comes to me as I move through these silent, vacant rooms, all open to the sky. The graceful arches of Tintern Abbey, the slow current of these lower reaches of the Wye, the deep hues of these hills embody for me an eloquence. In a young poet they shaped a voice that invites me to look inward, to cherish and celebrate the *spirit . . . that rolls through all things.* Two hundred years later, in a world paced for profit, the words inspired by this valley, these walls, give me pause.

JAN SHOEMAKER teaches world literature in Lansing, Michigan.

SYLVIA SHAW

The Prodigals

Christian Rohlfs.
*House in the
Mountains.*
Water-based pigments
on cream wove paper,
51½×65.3 cm., 1935.
The Detroit Institute
of Arts, Gift
of Mrs. Lillian Henkel
Haass and Walter
F. Haass in memory
of Reverend W. F. Haass.

NATHAN FIRST NOTICED HER, not because of her long auburn hair and expressive eyes, not because she looked all of twenty and walked with a cane, and not because her songbird voice was netted by apprehension; he locked onto her when she spoke one name: Egremont.

"I have to get to North Egremont tonight!" she insisted to the car rental agent.

"I'm sorry, Miss. This gentleman just took the last available car. Have you checked with Avis or . . ."

"They sent me to you!"

"I'm afraid the blizzard has turned everything upside down. All flights have been cancelled. We've had to service hundreds of stranded passengers. In another half hour or so Logan will shut down completely. I suggest you book into a hotel and wait out the storm."

"And spend Christmas alone? I'm expected in the Berkshires."

"I'm sorry, Miss."

The girl grasped the cane in one hand and her carry-on in the other. She set off resolutely. The exit door swung open for her, but she stopped abruptly in the open doorway. The storm blew her hair in wild eddies about her face. Nathan headed for her.

"I can take you as far as Stockbridge," he called out.

"Oh, thank you!" she answered without hesitation. Maybe she saw no taxis in the gloom, or perhaps she decided that riding with a stranger was less frightening than wandering the silent, eerie spaces of a major airport about to shut down.

They caught the last shuttle for the Hertz parking lot and stepped into a world grown silent despite the intensity of its activity. Boston lay buried under nearly two feet with more to come. Nathan's stomach tightened.

"This sure isn't California!" said the girl. "By the way, I'm Geneva Lloyd." She held out her hand across the hood of the car.

"Nathan Stone." He returned the strong handshake, hoping she wouldn't notice that he was trembling.

They worked their way through a city that seemed to have fallen asleep hours too early. A fleet of snow plows managed to keep one lane opened on the Massachusetts Turnpike. They would have to travel across the entire length of the state with dismal visibility. Nathan became anxious, his companion chatty. By the time they neared Worcester he could have written the definitive biography of Geneva Lloyd, twenty-one year old music student from the American Conservatory Theater of San Francisco. She told him about her parents' divorce, about the skiing accident that permanently damaged her right leg, about her father's recent move to the Berkshires and about her aspiration to play first-violin someday. Though her chatter was girlish and pleasant, it grated on his nerves.

"Enough about me," she exclaimed, folding her hands on her lap. "Tell me about you, Nate."

"Nathan. There's nothing to tell." He scowled at the speckled night. Damn! Why did it have to snow tonight of all nights? The question played like a stubborn refrain.

"Are you in school?"

"Yeah. Berkeley."

"Neat! And why are you here, Nate?"

"To visit the scene of my crime," he answered, not looking at her.

"What crime?"

He could feel those large eyes of hers. "I murdered my brother."

"You're kidding, right?"

He peered into the driving snow. Sturbridge lay ahead. Beyond that Palmer, Springfield, and all the other towns tugging on him, pulling him home to Stockbridge, where reality was not always as beatific as Norman Rockwell's vision of small-town life. He flicked on the radio. Muffled strains of Denver's *Take Me Home, Country Roads* tried to reach them through the murky night. Geneva turned down the volume.

"Why do you say you murdered your brother?"

"Because I did," he answered in a flat voice, eyes dead ahead. "Five years ago tonight."

"Why?" she asked in a voice as toned down as Denver's.

"Now that's a good question!" Nathan flung the words like acid in her face. "The truth is I don't know. I must have had a damn good reason to kill a twelve-year-old kid on the night before Christmas, don't you think? One moment he was sitting beside me all bubbly like you, the next he was a bloody mess!"

She had unfastened her seat belt during his tirade. Without warning she draped a leg over his lap and slammed down hard on the brake. The Mercury spun around and skidded off the empty road. Geneva screamed as they slammed into a snow embankment and came to an abrupt stop.

"Are you trying to kill us?!" he yelled.

She released her grip on his arm and punched it. "No! I just want you to stop! You're scaring me!"

Nathan put his hand on her shoulder and realized he was shaking as hard as she was.

He spoke gently, earnestly, in an attempt to soothe her. And he suddenly longed to kiss her, to lose himself in her soft hair, to hug her because he desperately needed to tell someone, anyone, especially this girl with an angel's face, what he carried inside. Instead he leaned back and closed his eyes. "It was all my fault," he told her quietly.

Nathan could no longer contain his guilt, no more than the sky could hold its ice and snow. Time doubled backed, and he was seventeen again, driving with Sam, trying to get home through a snow storm. But this time a young woman sat near him and tried to absolve him. "It wasn't your fault," she insisted after he'd told her the whole wretched story. "You were a young, inexperienced driver. Nate, look at me. Ice and snow are treacherous. Not you, Nathan!"

He stumbled out of the car and filled his lungs with the cold night. A snowplow stopped to help free the car from the snowbank, and they were on their way again, more than halfway across the state on a highway that seemed to belong to them alone. Nathan was still anxious about meeting his folks, especially his father, after four and a half years. But the confession had calmed him, leaving him free to actually enjoy the rest of the drive with Geneva. She would later say he talked a blue streak, boasting about his father.

"He's a minister like no other; you should hear him preach, especially when he talks about angels. No one portrays them quite like the good Reverend Jodiah Stone! No one can charge the Christmas story with such raw power, and terror, though he's normally the gentlest of men. *Angels,* Dad would remind us, *are supernatural beings. Never forget that in spite of their beauty they filled the shepherds with terror so stark, it crumpled them to the ground.*"

"I believe in angels, don't you?" Geneva interjected.

"No. I don't know. Sometimes my father gave me the uncanny feeling that he spoke from personal experience; that he somehow could transcend time and space for a few seconds at a time and be a shepherd visited by God's spirit; other times he was just like any other man his age: graying and sweating under his robes. But damn! I wish I had his faith, his granite firm, unwavering faith!"

JODIAH STONE WAS OFFICIATING, as he had for years, at the traditional Christmas Eve service. Most of his parishioners had braved the storm that night to hear him preach. He ascended the pulpit, but he didn't smile when he gazed into a sea of upturned faces. This particular Christmas Eve Jodiah Stone stood silent, unable to begin. When he finally spoke, he cast his sermon out like a great net, unsure what it would bring in.

"Every Christmas the Christian world makes a feeble attempt to commemorate an event so monumental, so astounding, that if we truly believed it, we would not be able to move or speak," he began. "We wouldn't comb the malls or bake or decorate or do any of the trivia that consumes us."

Jodiah Stone had all the gifts of the skilled orator, including physical presence. His gray hair had yielded silver, making his eyes seem all the more intensely blue. At six-feet-four inches, he remained impressively tall, though his shoulders sagged of late. His voice was orchestral in its range and power.

"My brethren," he tried again, "If we truly believed that God, who created the universe with its microcosms and macrocosms, actually came to us as a man and lived among us, that he conquered the hells that beset us, if we *truly* believed that there is more to this life than the impressions of our five senses, and that there really are beings who can materialize out of the darkness, terrifyingly, and speak to ordinary men and women, *if we believed . . .*"

His eyes shimmered in the subdued candle glow. His parishioners listened, enthralled by the sermon they had all come to count on, and none heard the question, the agonized pause. The minister leaned into the silence for an answer.

There is no God! No Messiah! Only death! He longed to shout. *All that we have is imagination and hope!*

But his love for his fellow humans breathed stronger than the need to speak the dismal truth that now haunted him. He could not deliver them into the pit he had slowly slid into himself since Samuel's death; he could not push them into the darkness where he found himself alone, trembling from helplessness. Hopelessness. So he launched into his rich repertoire and delivered the Christmas message with all his fabled power. After the service, he smiled and greeted each of his parishioners. His wife and children had gone home without him, not just to prepare for the family's traditional Christmas Eve dinner, but to prepare for Nathan. The prodigal son was returning home.

With the church silent and empty at last, the minister locked up. Slowly. He was in no hurry to rush home. He stepped outside and listened. The wind had stopped. Snow fell with silent persistence. He glanced down the street just as the power went out in Stockbridge and throughout the Berkshires. Every house along the village green faded into the night, except for the parish house. Stone's wife had insisted only two days earlier on buying battery operated candles for every window in the house. They now glowed softly, as reassuring as her smile. One by one, the tenuous glow of candles and lit fireplaces began to illuminate the other houses as well. In minutes the town with its elm trees and colonial houses slid back into the nineteenth century.

Not bothering to button his coat, Jodiah headed down the path connecting the church and the parish house. He entered a vestibule, its wide pine board floors worn down by generations of ministers and their large broods; the house smelled of roast lamb and mint glaze, of cinnamon and nutmeg. The dining room sideboard was covered with culinary wonders: a mince pie, a chocolate Yule log complete with meringue mushrooms, an apple tart, pecan rolls lush and sticky with caramel sauce, and the plum pudding that he would set ablaze after dinner. But everything irritated him: the sound of his daughter's voice, giddy with adolescent love, as she chatted about her boy friend; the repeated refrain of his youngest son: "Please, can I open just one before dinner?" Even his wife's cheeriness.

"Can you believe it! The lamb was done just as the power went out!" Millie Stone said happily as she put finishing touches on the table: Christmas napkin rings. As always, she set a place for Samuel though his chair had sat empty for five Christmases; she had done the same for Nathan ever since he left home. The table seated six comfortably. "Oh, Nathan called just before the power went out," she added with studied casualness.

"So? What did he say?"

"He's got a young woman with him; this is her first New England Christmas; her father just moved from California to North Egremont." Jodiah watched as she brought in a spare chair, one that did not match the others. "I told him not to even think about trying to get her there tonight; the town roads aren't plowed yet. She'll have to stay with us. He can get her home tomorrow after the plows have been through."

"He's bringing home some hitchhiker?"

"She's not a hitchhiker. They met at the airport."

Millie reached for Sam's place setting and hesitated, unaware of her husband's stare. He thought he could read her mind: "Won't the girl think us peculiar to set a place for Sam?" when in fact she was wondering, "Won't Nathan feel bad if he sees Sam's empty place?" Jodiah watched her vacillate. Then it seemed that she swooped down like a hawk in a barnyard and carried off Sam's place: he grabbed his jacket and headed out the rarely-used front door.

The night air stung his face. He headed around to the back of the house, not because he had anything to do there, but because he let his emotions lead him to the one place that might contain his anger, his gnawing resentment. The empty sheep pen. Looking up, Jodiah noticed that it had stopped snowing. He gazed up at the stars, luminous in a sky vast and magnificent. But as he hunched his shoulders against the cold air, he could not have known that it had only cleared in the wide circle that held the sheep pen and fenced paddock. Everywhere else, for a hundred miles in all directions, snow continued to fall, reshaping the landscape.

Jodiah entered the small barn. He could smell fresh hay, but he had to search his memory for the scent of animals. The sheep had been Sam's responsibility and joy; after the accident, Jodiah had sold the six of them. He claimed they were too much trouble. But in truth, it galled him that they with their dull eyes and dull minds should live to see the snow thaw and the trees blossom. So he sold them all to a man in South Egremont. Ironically, Millie went right on buying fresh hay. Perhaps she needed the scent of the hay as one more way to remember Samuel.

A gust of wind slammed the barn door hard against a wall of rough planks as he fumbled in the dark for the lantern and matches. Moments later a tenuous light fractured the frozen air. It lit a circle around him, keeping the rest of the barn in dark shadow. Jodiah

Stone held up the lantern as if to find the sheep or the boy who used to feed them. But he found only emptiness, the same void that haunted Sam's room—and Nathan's. He set the lantern down on the earthen floor.

Then he thought of his daughter Sarah and her pup of a boyfriend, of David anxious with childish greed and anticipation, and of Millie carting off Sam's place-setting, and he kicked the nearest hay bale, savagely, again and again, scratching the smooth leather of his dress shoes. He grasped the bale and flung it aside, then the next one and the one after that. Kicking and throwing them: one for Nathan, for driving too fast one icy night; another for slick roads and unforgiving trees; another for parishioners who look up to you; for role modeling that must be played out to the end; for God who makes promises and exacts too high a price; for a world without Sam and without God . . . and another bail for all the damn confusion in his head, his heart . . .

A FEW MILES AWAY Nathan pulled up in front of the clump of trees that killed his brother. He shined the high beams on them and approached softly. Alone. Afraid. The trees had grown in his imagination. These looked thin and ordinary, disconcertingly ordinary. Taking off a glove, he reached and touched the bark of the white oak. His fingers found the scar, the deep gash carved by the Chevy on impact. Nate felt his head droop to his arm. His despair suddenly fixed on a memory: the night Eunice-Ewe gave birth to her lamb. Sam had been beside himself with excitement. It was so cold that their breath hung crystallized in the air. "Dad! Nate! Look!" Sam cried excitedly. "She's getting ready! I can see smoke coming out of her!"

"Smoke, huh?" Jodiah had winked at Nathan.

Now the young man cried, overwhelmed by a guilt beyond the reach of forgiveness; beaten down because a whole lifetime could never ease the pain. Just down the road Jodiah Stone slumped to the ground and began to sob, emptying his soul in the small barn. When his sobs subsided and his thoughts staggered out, he realized what hurt most was everyone's return to normalcy. Everyone's forgetfulness.

Samuel was real, damn it! The father tugged on his hair and cried to the night. He was as real as this barn, as this hay, as this ground! And every day fewer people remember him.

Then he realized with a shudder that even he was beginning to forget; that his memories were often only snapshots. Exhausted, he sat on the ground and wiped his face with the back of his hand.

David was only five at the time of the accident. How can I expect him to remember his brother, he chastised himself. Samuel is just a name to him, some kind of tradition his parents pay homage to. David can't remember the soft innocence in Sam's eyes, or that he told absurd jokes and sang off key . . . .

A face, nebulous at first like morning mist, a face smooth with adolescence yet sparked with wisdom, emerged from the dark and approached him, unaware. Then it whispered something and Jodiah Stone *felt* an insight beyond words.

Reality is not predicated on memory. The fact that Sam is nearly forgotten after only five years does not make him any less real. The fault lies with us, with our imperfect powers of memory. How much more so when we are called upon to remember a man, however glorious, God Himself, if our collective memory must arch back two thousand years! Because I cannot bring the Lord to memory, is He any less real than Sam?

The lantern blew out. At that very moment, as Jodiah glanced over his shoulder, he saw him. A being who was both boy and man. Beautiful. With Samuel's eyes. An angel whose smile told him even as he vanished, *you see? Terror is only momentary, if at all.*

"Sam!"

In the empty barn, Jodiah Stone began to pray, to surrender his disbelief to a force stronger than anger or despair. Another voice, stronger than his son's, a voice he had known all along, spoke soundlessly:

"If you can believe, all things are possible for him who believes."

To which Jodiah whispered the words of another desperate father, a plea culled from the depths of his soul, "Lord, I believe; help my unbelief."

He closed his eyes and tipped back his head until it rested against the wall. It was then that he became aware of a pleasant warmth and of a smell: the comforting scent of animals, manure, and fresh hay. There were voices, low and murmuring, indistinguishable. And then a sound, so clear it resonated from the top rafters to the dirt floor. The crying of an infant.

Jodiah felt a shock run through his body, the sharp thrill of fear, a fear that kept his eyes clamped shut and that sent the blood pounding to his ears. Without opening his eyes he knew that the barn was no longer square in shape; that it held large animals, and people murmuring words from an ancient language. The baby cried until his mother brought him to her breast. Jodiah was no longer afraid. He knew that to open his eyes would dispel the moment, this overlapping of experience separated by time and space yet compressed here, fleetingly, for him if he didn't open his eyes, if he only allowed himself to listen, to experience it, and to believe.

He was a man in a dark, cold barn, his feet numb, his face wet with tears; an angel guided his thoughts as he traveled inward, to that central place that transcends all time and space. He perceived for the first time that there is no emptiness, only a vast, magnificent network of spirits and angels who work continuously to connect humanity to God. And Jodiah Stone grasped the parallel between his memory and the collective human memory of a night, a child, a reality no less real than the birth, the death, and the resurrection of his son. He listened inwardly with eyes shut, even as the scent and sounds became fainter, until they too vanished into the mist of his breath and his prayer.

When he stepped out of the sheep pen and closed the gate behind him, Jodiah gazed into a mysterious sky. Snow fell from inscrutable heights. He suddenly felt the impulse to catch every snowflake, to shout, to fly into the sable depths. Headlights probed the dark. They connected him to the car that had just pulled into the driveway. Shielding his eyes, he stared into the beams. Without shutting them off, Nathan stepped out of the car.

Nathan, who had rehearsed his lines throughout the drive, who labored under the guilt of survival, who believed Samuel to be his father's favorite and himself a lesser light, Nathan who had stayed away for fear of this very encounter, of seeing a distant look that asked, why are you here instead of your brother? Nate who could no longer remember his carefully planned greeting, watched his father step into the light and hold out his arms to him, with a look of joy so intense, so penetrating, that he rushed down the hill into that embrace.

SYLVIA SHAW says, "I first read Swedenborg's *Heaven and Hell* in college—unbelieving, intrigued, awestruck. It has been thirty years since that first encounter with this remarkable book. In writing 'The Prodigals', I focused on two ideas: that angels are human beings who once lived in our world, and that heaven with all its wonders is indeed within us, in what Swedenborg calls that 'central or highest level' in each of us: 'This central or highest level can be called God's gateway to the angel or the mortal, His essential dwelling within us'"(*Heaven and Hell*, paragraph 39).

JOAN D. STAMM

The Way
of Flowers

W. Joe Innis. *The
Standing Blue Vase.*
Acrylic on canvas,
28×37 in.
From the collection
of Dr. Takaaki Nakamoto,
Japan.

BEYOND THE FRINGE OF URBAN FARMLAND where radish and rice
fields meet pine-forested hills, stands an ancient temple in northwestern Kyoto. The birthplace of the *Shingon* sect, it was founded by

the famous saint, scholar, and poet Kukai in the ninth century, and it was also the summer palace of Emperor Saga, who loved and preserved the arts. These two influential masters ushered in the Heian Period, a golden era of artistic and cultural achievement lasting three hundred years.

Today, eleven hundred years later, *Daikaku-ji* is not only a prominent historical temple, but the international headquarters of the Saga Goryu School of Ikebana. The word *ikebana,* commonly translated as Japanese flower arranging, literally means "to preserve living flowers," or "to preserve the essence of nature in a vase." Through learning a complex system of rules, artistic principles, and symbolic meaning, and by observing the beauty and quietude of nature, the *ikebana* practitioner strives to incorporate Buddhist concepts of peace, harmony, and reverence into daily life. Pursuit of the spiritual through the art of flower arranging is the greater study of *Kado,* the Way of Flowers.

When Emperor Saga sailed around Osawa pond, a tiny lake on the grounds of *Daikaku-ji,* he spotted chrysanthemums blooming on one of its two islands; he picked the flowers and arranged them in three tiers, depicting heaven, earth, and man. Thus originated the Saga school of *ikebana.* The Osawa pond, surrounded by cherry trees, pagodas, and stone statues of Buddha, provides a peaceful shoreline where visitors stroll and stare and feed its fat carp. In Saga's time, the phoenix-prowed boats sailed these waters while the Heian aristocrats languished under the boat's silk awnings alongside ladies dressed in twelve shades of silk kimonos with hair so long it brushed their toes.

In the gardens of the *Daikaku-ji,* centuries-old stone bridges are thick with lichen, under Japanese maples turning crimson red. The temple gate with its mammoth wooden door and black iron hinges leads to inner corridors that spread deep into the heart of the temple. The walkways enhanced with carved balustrades and gold hinges zigzag across moss gardens and end at shrines, viewing verandahs, or dark corners. The temple, connected to the school and student dormitories by stone paths or meandering and embellished corridors, presents a disorienting and mysterious triangular layout. *Shingon* Buddhism is a sect that practices chanting, visualization, and special body postures: techniques for achieving enlightenment.

Students bow their heads to the mat. *The shoji* doors open and a parade of monks files into the room, each one wearing a black silk kimono with a white under-kimono falling in a tube-shape to the ankles and white *tabi* (opaque split-toed silk stockings). Each monk has a saffron drape uniformly placed over the left shoulder. At the collar, where layers of white, black, and saffron meet in a clean flat fold, a wooden fan sticks up like a carp fin.

The monks take their places within the inner sanctuary, a separate area cordoned off by a low black railing. Images of *Dainichi Nyorai* (the universal Buddha), *Shogonkas* (formal flower arrangements common to Buddhist shrines), and glittering gold objects that symbolize the radiance of enlightenment adorn the altar. As the priests sit on their heels and arrange their long billowy sleeves, the only sound is the rustle of silk falling in graceful folds. Simultaneously they arrive at correct and poised postures, and a young monk begins a ritual of transporting a sacred text from the altar to the presiding monk. A novitate begins chanting the *Hannya Haramita Shin-gyo.* He is joined by the full-throated warbling of others. The deep melodic male voices, synchronized in rhythmic tones and cadences, provide a setting for the Three Mystic Practices for achieving enlightenment: sacred body postures, cultivation of faith through meditative concentration, and divine chanting.

At the end of the service, the sacred text goes back to the altar, the silk robes rustle into position, and the monks file out.

Raked, swirling shapes in the white rock gardens are illuminated by the bluish light of sunrise as each day begins. In front of Japanese black pines trained into long sweeping arches are dozens of six-foot chrysanthemums pruned into three-tiered configurations and grouped in patterns of white, yellow, and magenta: the heaven, earth, and man principle of *ikebana*.

In the school cafeteria, ikebana students enjoy the subtle flavors and delicate textures of Japanese food, which complement the discipline of morning service and flower arranging. The class begins with an outline of twenty-eight prohibitions for choosing and pruning plant material. For example,

- Don't use rice stalks or chestnuts or other plants that are food crops. This only applies to traditional arrangements, not modern.
- Don't arrange flowers without knowing their names. *This shows lack of respect for the plant.*
- Don't use branches that are entangled, for *it reminds us of rebellion against one's parents and goes against the teaching of Confucius.*
- Don't use branches that point straight up to heaven; don't use branches that point to earth, our mother; and don't use flowers that point to each other. *Pointing is considered rude.*
- Don't use branches that hang down, for they do not look brisk.

- Don't use branches that are even, for they will be in conflict with each other. *Short and long, yin and yang.*

In a low black bowl the teacher places a corn plant leaf at a forty-five degree angle, making sure the stems are positioned together without any gaps between them. She places a dracaena leaf and freesia blossom next to the corn leaf. Then she de-thorns and prunes a quince branch and replaces the corn plant leaf with this new material. Her actions are confident; her movements easy and graceful. When she is satisfied with the results she chooses a mat the color of sunflowers to go under the container for display.

In contemplating such a flower arrangement the viewer is as still and balanced as the flowers.

In the *Shingon* teaching, all persons are intrinsically enlightened, but they are deluded until the practice of such a discipline as Ikebana recalls the enlightened state into consciousness. Artistic creations are Buddhas in their own right: nature, art, and religion are one. Lessons continue as further prohibitions are put forth:

- Don't point flowers so that they cover each other. *Each flower should shine in individual glory.*
- Don't have two branches going the same direction. *One path is all one can follow.*
- Flowers should not face the viewer like a mirror. *Narcissism is not good.*
- Don't place two leaves directly opposite each other. Prune one or the other. *Competition can turn into a battle.*
- Don't place flowers as if they are holding each other. *Stand alone, strong and independent.*

Once these lessons are established, the class turns to the task of *morimono,* one of five variations under *Bunjinka. Bunjin* means "cultured person" and comes from *Bunjinga,* a Chinese drawing school introduced to Japan in the eighteenth century. The *Bunjinka* style incorporates freedom of composition and playfulness of design while still maintaining balance and harmony. Arrangements in this style are given titles, taken from either the symbolic meaning of flowers—pine as eternal youth, rose as everlasting spring—or from old Chinese folk tales and poems.

In an ancient storeroom, wood beams, thick as tree trunks, cracked and dusty with age, handmade ceramic vases and *dai* (wood and bamboo platforms) are made and kept.

Rectangle-shaped *dai* (square shapes are considered uninteresting—too symmetrical) are used to arrange vegetables in the *morimono* style. A Japanese pumpkin is put off to one side, while color combinations are considered. Stacks of carrots and peppers and mushrooms are placed asymmetrically in groups of three and five. Bitter is good with sweet, green is good with red—in the practice of yin and yang, the balance of opposites makes a harmonious whole. As a *morimono* on display is finished, it is named and offered for display. Again, contemplation leads to a rare and illusive moment; peace returns: the compositional whole encompasses desire and the desire not to desire as well as the permission to desire.

The last lesson is on the religious roots of the Saga school and the six elements of *Shingon* Buddhism: earth, water, wind, fire, space, and knowledge. Symbolically, these six elements embody aspects of Buddha nature, each one perfect unto itself but not existing apart from the whole. Earth depicts mountains and prairies, but also bones and muscles; water represents oceans and rivers, but also blood and tears; fire is at once sunshine and body heat; wind symbolizes breath. To arrange flowers is to personify these elements. Use long sweeping willow branches for fire and water, for example, or a pruned azalea branch for wind, leathery ferns for earth, pink amaryllis for space, and yellow lilies with cedar for knowledge. The colors create harmony, the six elements work as a dynamic unit, the whole radiates oneness of body and mind.

On national holidays the temple opens to the public and throngs of tourists come to see the chrysanthemums: the national flower and symbol of royalty. The sightseers stand on the verandah over Osawa Pond. The centuries-old planks creak beneath slippered feet as visitors move among giant chrysanthemums—heaven, earth, man; white, yellow, magenta—repeating in patterns on the edges of raked stones. A raven calls out from the top of a Japanese black pine, and mourning doves coo under tiled eaves oozing with the smell of sandalwood incense, the smell of peace and calm and reverence. As the light filters through orange leaves of split-leaf maple, it creates a burning bush of the Orient.

JOAN D. STAMM is a freelance writer with a master's degree in fine arts in writing and literature from Bennington College. During her two years in Japan, she edited speeches, books, and articles on the peace potential of the yakumo-goto, a sacred Shinto musical instrument. Currently, she lives in the Pacific Northwest where she works with Southeast Asian and East African refugees, and studies *ikebana* and Zen Buddhism.

SUSAN PICARD

Beyond the Blue

THEY SAY THAT YOU CAN'T BE IN TWO PLACES AT THE SAME TIME. But my daughter was; I saw her. Picture a small, thin, thirteen-year-old girl astride a sixteen-hand horse. She has an achingly beautiful face, with a child's small features and a child's large eyes, though there is something about the fullness of her lips that suggests the woman she will become. Sticking out from the back of her riding hat are wisps of golden hair that she won't bring under control as the other girls have. She is waiting to enter the ring in her first rated show—she has ridden in only a few, unrated, shows—and her small, child's hands, gloved for the show, are clenching and unclenching her reins. She is the first to compete in her class.

The unevenly braided mane of her horse sprouts wisps, too. This thirteen-year-old lacks the long experience of the other girls here in grooming their horses for the ring. The mane is not her horse's only point of departure from equine elegance: his butt and his neck are skinny, and his tail is regrettably sparse. He is a flea-bitten gray, and the term, in his case, is apt. But he is his scraggly best for the show, curried and buffed to a gleam by the girl hours ago in the pre-dawn dark. His name is Duke of Earl.

Because she is my daughter, I know that all the wisps don't have to be on display. I offered to fix her hair just moments ago, but she refused the offer. Earlier this morning, I offered to pay her trainer to braid Duke's mane; she refused that offer, too. And because this girl is my daughter, I can tell you something about her. She is shy, tentative, unsure of herself in many situations. It is remarkable to me that she wants to compete at all. She must love to ride, because she isn't

John Cavanaugh. *In Search of Motion.* Bronze, 18½ inches, 1983. Swann's Way Gallery, Washington, D.C. Photograph by John Elsbree.

one to draw attention to herself, especially in front of strangers. In front of judges. My daughter's name is Mattie.

So now Mattie enters the ring looking like the two-bit equestrienne that she is, sitting stiffly on her two-bit horse. Standing ringside watching her are two older girls that she knows from school. These girls both grew up on sprawling gentlemen's farms, and they both own and ride expensive horses. They've been riding expensive horses, and their parents have been paying expensive trainers, since they were very young; each is years beyond her first rated show.

Duke and Mattie approach the first jump, and Duke goes over easily. Mattie canters him toward the second jump. Have I mentioned that Duke does not really *like* to jump? He has been a good first horse for Mattie, a tractable mount that she can trust to stay within her control, but Duke has never met a jump with gusto. So while I am disappointed when he stops just short of the second jump, I can't say I'm surprised.

The blue ribbon, the symbol of performance success, is now, in every likelihood, out of Mattie's reach. But she might still take a third, or maybe even a second. This is a class for green novices, after all, and the riders who follow her may fare no better than she. I see her clamp her legs tight around Duke's girth to urge him onward as they come out of the turn to approach the second jump for the second time. I sense that she wants Duke to gather momentum enough to be unable to stop. It's a good strategy, I think, even though Duke is probably moving a little faster than the judges want to see. The horse and rider should be relaxed, not rushed.

Mattie, too, must think her strategy is a good one. She must be fully expecting Duke to leave the ground, because when Duke stops dead-on-a-dime at the second jump, Mattie, unprepared, does not. She soars effortlessly past Duke's head and lands with a little *thwump* on the ground. Her mini-flight was executed with grace: I can see that she is not hurt.

I hurt. I hurt for her.

The two older girls that she knows drift away from the ring. They are sensitive to remove themselves from the scene of Mattie's disgrace; conversation will be awkward when she comes out of the ring. A ribbon now is out of the question. The competition is over for Mattie and Duke. It remains merely for Mattie to re-mount Duke and circle him once more for their third and final attempt at the jump. This third jump is a courtesy to allow the rider to take back control from the horse, to keep the horse from having the final say about where and when it will jump.

Mattie brings Duke up to the jump at just the right gait, but she digs her heels sharply into his flanks as they reach it. Her heels in his flanks are of no consequence to Duke, and he stops dead again. The ride has been an utter failure. During my admittedly short stint as a riding mom, I've never seen a horse refuse the same jump three times srunning. Poor, poor Mattie! What am I going to say or do to comfort her, I wonder, trying to breathe away the tightness constricting my heart as I wait for her to leave the ring. I hate this moment; I hate how hard it hurts.

But now Mattie is circling Duke for a fourth go at the jump. There is a startled murmur among the spectators: what is she doing? Doesn't she know that she has to get out of the ring? Her trainer, standing near the gate, calls out in a loud stage whisper, "Mattie! You can come out of the ring now!"

I draw in my breath. What is Mattie doing? Why is she jumping again? Breaking the rules is not her style, and breaking the rules for all to see is uncharacteristic to an alarming degree. Is something wrong with her? Did she hit her head when she fell? Has she forgotten how to count? What is wrong!?

But Mattie is cantering Duke straight at the jump as if for the first and not for the fourth time, as if with no expectation of failure. She is poised and relaxed and makes no special effort that I can discern to urge Duke over. She is riding as if the past and the future do not exist: as if the history of the last two minutes never occurred, and as if the future holds no consequences for her transgression. Duke knows the drill, all of us watching know the drill; and so Duke's abrupt refusal yet again to take the jump seems both inevitable and rightly scripted.

And now what comes to my awareness as I watch Mattie circle Duke for the fifth time is the understanding that Mattie isn't *here*. Yes, she is in the ring, riding before my eyes; and no, she isn't in this ring anymore. Her absence from the ring in front of my eyes is the reason that she doesn't hear her trainer who is now waving at her and hissing in desperation, "Mattie! Come out of the ring! You have to come out of the ring!"

Mattie is poised and relaxed because she is riding her horse in a place beyond the ribbons and rules, beyond all of us watching her, beyond judges and judgment itself, in a place where there is only herself, the horse, and the jump. There is not, in this other place, an attachment to outcome. Her task is to bring Duke to the jump with the skill and intent to take him over. But it is of no matter if he does not jump. If he does not jump, it becomes her task to try again. There is no room for ego in this place, no room for fear of failure or for shame. This place is filled to its infinite bounds with rider, horse, and jump, and with the immediacy of doing what is to be done: riding to the jump. It seems, in this place, that Mattie can ride forever.

Tears are streaming down my face and I am laughing like a goon. I know what I am witnessing is profound. Mattie has become my own Olympic athlete, transcending her earthly limitations of time and space to ride among the gods. I am fiercely proud of this small, shy, beautiful girl with the wisps of hair sticking out of her hat. I am fiercely proud that she has found a way to ride her scruffy horse away from the place in the ring where she is a failure to another place where she is the ideal rider, bearing down on the jump with only the perfection of the moment. That transcendent place, where all of us long to be.

BACK IN THE PLACE OF RIBBONS AND RULES, Mattie and Duke never completed the jump. They were led to the gate by the judge who, according to regulation, had gone in to get them out. A competition was in progress there, and another competitor at the gate was waiting her turn to enter the ring.

There was no ribbon from the judge for Mattie. But there was, as she rode from the ring, a ribbon of sorts: a sweet, surprising crescendo of long and loud applause.

SUSAN PICARD is marketing manager for the Swedenborg Foundation in West Chester, Pennsylvania.

PART IV

The Other Side of the Looking Glass

A Different Place

RELIGIOUS ECSTASY,
personal relationships,
life purposes
are pursued as amalgams of reality and symbol.
The perceived reality may be indeed very different
from what is presented in both cases;
but symbols partake of the reality they symbolize.
When we experience the reality
before we find its meaning in a symbol,
we may often find ourselves in that uncertain state
of knowing and not knowing,
of rubbing our eyes as if to clear our perception.
When it clears,
symbols that have haunted us—
perhaps an ecstatic vision
or a charging hippopotamus
—come alive.

Sometimes, the hard part
is separating the symbol
from our expectations.
"Mirrors of Meaning" provides
some easily recognized fingerposts
for that difficult task.

—ROBERT H. KIRVEN

SUZANNE FREEMAN

Gila River Sycamores

Bare April sycamores
flash their startling, bone-white bark,
a grove of fantastical, ghostly shapes
stark against the red-walled canyon.
A woodpecker's tiny drumbeat,
the constant hum of river
lend rhythm to dancing skeletons,
giants that loom and list in ridiculous poses
while branches twist and grab at sky.
One can see a tree adopt
a Shiva stance,
another plays the cello
of a fallen pine.
Two more attempt a multi-limbed embrace,
year upon year,
impossible lovers.

How many miles
of shallows and sand, how many centuries
upon the dance-floor of sparkling rock, mint, and mullein
before I would shed
the leaves of inhibition
and join the austere choreography?

SUZANNE FREEMAN is a writer who lives in the hill country of Texas.

I.E. STEELE

Invention of the Paper Clip

queued for a bus
a man bends
his horizon
end to end
and over itself again

riding to work
he toys with what will not break
bent repeatedly
unlike principles
or love

in the chain of pawns
bent on advancement
he permutates paper
wherries cast to the winds
clipped with his wire sail

he re-pinions commuters
fleeing five o'clock shadows
as his journey homeward snakes
through twilight's shedding skin

he braces leaves to boughs
smoke to chimneys
wishes to maverick stars
and eclipses the sun with moonbow

his will refashions the universe
until the shortest distance
between two points
is his design

I.E. STEELE, born in New York City, holds a bachelor's of art degree from Hunter College. He has authored poetry and fiction in over twenty journals, a poetry chapbook published by *Pulp,* a story broadcast over the BBC World Service, one novel, and several plays.

WALTER R. CHRISTIE

The Icon of Sophia

The icons were born out of spirit; their chief characteristic is timelessness. Utterly calm, they are a "threshold" for the reverent soul, a window opening upon the world of spiritual archetypes, "guides" to the spirit-beings they represent.[1]

ABOVE THE BATTLEMENTS OF THE ANCIENT RUSSIAN CITY of Novgorod rises the great cathedral of St. Sophia. Here on a smooth wall, fifteenth-century priests produced the image of an eternal woman in a red gown seated upon the throne of wisdom. Gazing serenely outward toward struggling humanity, St. Sophia effortlessly clasps the staff of divine intention which rests on the earth and points toward the "starry script of the eternal." [2] Green-gold rays of hope stream from Sophia toward the Christian symbols of John the Baptist on her left and the Virgin Mary on her right. Above her, Jesus Christ rests in cosmic glory, and higher still angels surround the word of God in the form of an open book. [3]

For the Russian mystic and philosopher Vladimir Soloviev, the holy icon of Sophia, the All Wisdom of God, was the symbol and likeness of an Eternal Friend. Sophia had visited him three times in visions; and thereafter the stunning saint occupied his thoughts. He describes the icon's inspiring power:

> This majestic female figure—receiving adoration from the last representative of the Old Testament and the pregenitress of the New Testament, is the actual, pure, perfect humanity. It is the most exalted, all-encompassing form, one with God from all eternity, and in the temporal process finding oneness with Him

Head of a Female Saint
(from the church
of Hagiou Staurou,
near Jerusalem). Fresco
transferred to panel,
14¾×10⅝ in.,
Byzantine, twelve
to fourteenth century.
Museum of Fine Arts,
Boston, M. Theresa
B. Hopkins Fund.

and uniting to Him everything that exists. Beyond any doubt this is the true significance of this majestic Being. [4]

Hoping to hold back the nihilistic tide at the turn of the century that threatened Russia's cultural foundation, Soloviev prayed to the icon for world peace, for the union of all religions, and for the manifestation of divine humanity. [5]

At age 22, Soloviev, having already first met Sophia when he was nine, had published his ideas about positivism and was working to define the philosophy and theology of Sophia's actions within the human soul and society. [6] He lectured often about an approaching world theocracy via the unification of all churches and peoples, and he wrestled with the theological and philosophical impasses raised by the positivists, who denied supersensible reality. Autumn 1875 found Soloviev in the British Museum library studying Sophia and her various historical manifestations, such as the Egyptian Isis. Dissatisfied with mere study, he longed for a reunion and found himself daydreaming about the great joy his Eternal Friend had brought him in the Moscow cathedral. In the glow of this memory, he sud-

denly sensed her presence and exuberantly called to her in his mind
to ask why she had not appeared to him again.

> Hardly had I thought these words
> When suddenly all was filled with golden
> azure,
>
> And you were there in heavenly radiance;
> There I saw your face, your face alone![7]

Grateful for the sight of Sophia's face, Soloviev begged his
Eternal Friend to reveal the fullness of her noble image as she had
when he was a child. "Be in Egypt!" Sophia's voice responded within
his mind, and Soloviev obeyed, immediately booking passage to
Cairo where he discovered the dangers of the naive pursuit of an inner image in an unknown terrain. Not knowing how to proceed, he
was forced to spend several weeks in Cairo where he studied Coptic
and waited. Finally one evening "in the stillness of the silent night,
Like a cool breeze I heard the whisper, 'I'm in the desert, you'll surely find me there.'[8]

Impulsively Soloviev dressed in his long black London coat,
gloves, and tall silk hat and set off into the desert. Unsure of where
he was going and totally unprotected, he was captured by Bedouins
and taken prisoner for ransom or death. His appearance was so
strange, however, that his captors thought he was the devil and let
him go to wander and starve as night fell and jackals began to howl.
Totally lost, Soloviev lay on a cold dune while despair congealed in
his heart. Thoughts of death flew through his mind until a gentle
whisper urged him, "Sleep, my poor friend!"

> I fell asleep, and upon awaking
> Celestial vault and earth with roses breathed.
> In your radiance of heavenly glory,
> Your eyes aflood with azure fire,
> Shine forth like ethereal dawning
> Of cosmic creation's primal day.
> Everything that was, and ever will be
>
> One moment's fleeting glance encompassed;
> Distant forests, seas and rivers far below me,
>
> Snowy mountain-heights, enwrapped in
> shimmering blue.
>
> I gazed upon it all, and all was fair,
> In form of Womanhood, embracing all in one:

The infinite encircled there, yet limitless
Before me and within me—You alone![9]

Like his philosopher model Boehme, Soloviev was certain that
the divine origin of his visions of Sophia was absolute, that knowledge inspired by his visions was true. Dan Merkur, author of *Gnosis,
An Esoteric Tradition of Mystical Visions and Unions,* defines this yok-
ing of vision, knowledge, and certainty as "gnosis," a special catego-
ry of knowledge recognized in Western mystical and esoteric practices. Gnosis, whether ushered in by image, idea, or inner voice, is experienced by the seeker as part of the divine order. To know gnostically is to directly participate with the divine.

> . . . a paired use of visionary and unitive experiences, dependent
> for the most part on active imagination, constituted the gnosis,
> "knowledge," at the mystical core of the gnostic trajectory in
> Western esotericism from late antiquity to modern times.[10]

Merkur borrows the term 'active imagination' from C.G. Jung,
who believed that religious symbols and knowledge arise from the
deepest level of our psyche, the collective unconscious. Memories of
thousands of years of biological and cultural evolution are organized
here into patterns (archetypes) that are visually accessible and symbolically meaningful.[11] In the spiritual person, active imagination
acknowledges these deep images as symbols of the divine.

In Jungian terms, Soloviev's active imagination was unfolding,
mediated by an inner center of divine knowledge that Jung called the
Self. [12] Passionate aspiration and hard work led Soloviev to divine
gnosis accompanied by such certainty that he went to Egypt. He fled
into the desert, lost his mindfulness, and regressed. Captured and released, starving and freezing in the dark ocean of dunes, Soloviev was
in great need of his Eternal Friend. But Sophia did not appear at first
when he was in such a willful, regressed, and demanding state of
mind. Instead Sophia's voice directed Soloviev to surrender to sleep.
In the sleep world close to the archetypal ground of being Soloviev
felt the potential wholeness of the psyche, and with it a primordial
change. He was aroused to an unexpectedly full union with Sophia.

For seconds, the Sophia vision in the desert was corporeal, a dazzling vast extra psychic reality, and Soloviev merged with her, soared
with her, and was inseparable from her. Boundaries between self and
Other disappeared, and she was everywhere, and he was everywhere
in her. She was the planet and every stone, plant, and creature on the
planet. She was the sweep of the cosmos and the drop of dew on the
flower. Gnostically prepared, with active imagination unbounded,
Soloviev flung his arms wide to receive the full power of her visionary gift. The dyadic devotional relationship between lover and

Beloved, between self and Other,[13,14] is beautifully portrayed in Soloviev's mystical experiences with Sophia, where his Eternal Friend becomes and remains the iconic doorway to the self and to God.

Studying infant cognitive processes, Kenneth Wright theorizes that sight is the primary creator of the psychological experience of form and identity.[15] The human infant's growing knowledge of a separate self takes shape when the gaze of another, usually the mother, meets the child's emerging experience of being. The face becomes the aboriginal icon, a protosymbol on which all future formed psychological experience will be built. Of course, mothers are not icons, and must come and go. To avoid the pain of abandonment, the infant creates symbols to serve as substitutes for her presence. Applying Wright's ideas, the mother's face meeting her son's existence, and the symbols Soloviev formed to represent this gaze in its absence, became the template for his experience of God.

The phenomenon of a face that returns our gaze is a main feature of iconographic religious art. By the symbolic perfection of its particular visage, the icon can appear to look back at the beholder. When eye meets eye, the beholder's heart and imagination open, and the emerging reality is flooded with emotional fullness.

Iconic gazing is practiced in many of the great religious traditions. Diana Eck describes the Hindu darshan:

The central act of Hindu worship, from the point of view of the lay person, is to stand in the presence of the deity and to behold the image with one's own eyes to see and be seen by the deity.[16]

In Western Christian contemplative tradition, the gnostic spark of divine knowledge experienced within the heart is founded on this primal interactional gaze. Meister Eckhart, a fourteenth-century Rhineland mystic, describes "the eye of the heart"[17] by saying that "the eye with which I see God is the eye with which God sees me."[18]

Soloviev's whole life as well as his method of contemplating spiritual reality, was iconic. From his birth his mother and his governess were so expressive, sensuous, imaginative, and symbolically evocative that they became flesh and blood extensions of the mysterious Other, the Sophia aspect of divinity latent in the human psyche and at work in the cosmos. They carried the power of Mother-as-Mystery well into his adulthood. Mother/Sophia was both muse and oracle, supporting constant imaginative symbolic formation.

An aura of love and magical excitation such as that cultivated by Soloviev's mother is not necessarily conducive to developing gnostic mysticism. Extreme creativity can possibly produce a dependent, regressed individual incapable of leaving the nest. Most developmental theories remind us that the soothing reality of an omnipresent mother must fail in some way so that separation can take place. Some irritation must occur in the developing consciousness, and the battleground between the wish to embrace the feminine and to differentiate from it, is the edge of what Jung called individuation.[19]

Sophia did not always appear when wished for. In many mystical individuals a perturbed mood set the stage for illumination.[20,21] Transformative religious experience often arises from the torment of a spiritual call that seems impossible to answer. At the point of ultimate impossibility, the seeker finds God.[22] At a critical moment both unconscious darkness and bodily pain dissolve, and the psyche opens to remarkable images, thoughts, and voices of an unseen reality which can transform the tormented spiritual heart.

Jungian analyst Robert Johnson's book *Lying with the Heavenly Woman* identifies feminine aspects of the human psyche, illuminating Soloviev's spiritual development. Feminine "noble elements of feeling, wisdom and relatedness" include the personal mother, the mother complex, the mother archetype, the anima, and Sophia.[23]

The personal mother is "a finite personal being with all her characteristics, idiosyncracies, virtues, and faults," while the mother complex Johnson defines as a cluster of urges and behaviors that reflect the "wish to regress to infancy again and to be taken care of."[24,25] A third maternal as part of the psyche, the mother archetype, serves the functions of supporting growth and self realization. In Soloviev's case his personal mother clearly merged with a powerful mother archetype.

The anima, as described by Jung, is a development of the inner feminine and serves as an intermediary between conscious personality and the depths of the collective unconscious.[26] Soloviev's first meeting with his Eternal Friend carried elements of the mother archetype and anima, fused with memories of his mother, his governess, and clearly demonstrated Sophianic qualities. Although a mother archetype offers sustenance and protection, and an anima points the way to a more inspiring reality, Soloviev required the balanced, interactive power of Sophia to dissolve his regression and lift him to a higher level of consciousness. When the Eternal Friend appeared, she was a being from heaven, and immediately Soloviev became more heavenly. In that moment, his consciousness was radically changed.

Sophia operates through the outer world as well as the psyche. In Soloviev's childhood vision in the Moscow cathedral, for example, she was manifest subliminally within the cathedral service as well as in her startling visionary appearance. The evocative colors and symbolism of the church interior, the archaic smells of incense, the ceremonial behavior of the priests, the magical words of the scripture, were aspects of Sophia that blended with the aspirations of a spiritually-inclined boy raised in an atmosphere of feminine mystery and imagination. The presence of divine grace and human disturbance evoked Soloviev's Sophia archetype. This illuminating inner image and richly textured outer environment focused and channeled the young boy's energy into a bright mystical vision, giving Soloviev a glimpse of the beauty of a transcendental world that would occupy the rest of his life.

Most of the lessons we might learn from Soloviev's experience he could have taught us himself, for he was an intellectually-schooled, modern individual, who, near the end of the nineteenth century, was dealing with the same issues of thought and social order that we struggle with a century later, including complexities, pitfalls, the reliability of love as an evolutionary force and as a divine guide.

As a poet, he understood that as living creatures, we see the world through our own perceptual capacities, developmental paths, cultural symbols, and interpretations. Spiritual knowledge, or gnosis, must be glimpsed through a human lens. Revelation expresses itself through images familiar and dear to us and through timeless symbols and myths common to our culture and experience. Although the symbol may remain similar in each age, its gnostic content expands to keep pace with the development of science and thought.

Iconic reality, the power of eye-to-eye engagement with a passionately loved, fascinating object of devotion is encoded in our genes and early childhood development. This mode of knowing offers a symbol that gazes back, becoming a doorway to an invisible world within the psyche and transcendent beyond the stars. As the icon returns one's gaze, a union takes place between seer and seen. This reciprocal relationship widens the awareness of life's mystery, increasing compassion and reflecting a pattern of invisible love that unifies reality and animates the heart.

Iconic reality opens an interior faculty for seeing. The foundation is ordinary perception, but the source of images is beyond the consciousness of the perceiver. Operating through images, the active imagination, or Imagination, is distinguished from ordinary fantasy to emphasize its supra-sensible source and its autonomy from instinct-dominated forces like wish-fulfillment.[27,28] The science of Imagination was active in the Western Renaissance in such spiritually inspired figures as Boehme, Swedenborg, Blake, Goethe, and Soloviev.

NO MATTER HOW STRANGE IT MAY APPEAR, the iconic doorway is real. Although a primordial symbol such as Sophia, as an expression of the Eternal Feminine, may look no different phenomenologically than a Neolithic goddess. In the human psyche, however, these archaic qualities are chosen not to highlight primitiveness, but instead speak to the symbol's centrality, its universality, its ability to hold figure and ground in a single, indivisible whole.[29]

As Soloviev knelt before the icon, he sought this indivisibility, for he feared that in the West an imbalance was close to destroying the spiritual supports of civilization. He believed that only Sophia, the eternal feminine, could save us from nihilism and despair. The overly rational, nonrelational thinking of materialist philosophers and survival-of-the-fittest social theorists was paving the way for dark forces to erupt in the twentieth century, forces that would drive people to a frenzy of material acquisitiveness, class struggle, and ultimately world war.

Soloviev died in 1900, and a century later we have experienced and survived many of the horrors he feared. In the meantime, citizens of industrialized countries have been complicit with the sacrilegious processes he anticipated, embracing a global economy that threatens the existence of millions of species, exploits marginalized peoples, and challenges the ecological integrity of our beautiful planet. This destruction continues despite the progress of the environmental movement, an increasing concern for the rights of women and children, the revival of Goddess and Native American traditions, and the rising interest in mysticism, holism, health, and healing.

Acknowledging the need for direction from a higher realm, Vladimir Soloviev's mystical experience is illuminating. While seeing the world through his eyes and maintaining the tension between mysticism and postmodern rationality, we stand in the presence of Sophia and are transformed. To see differently is to be different.

Now at the end of the twentieth century, Soloviev invites us to look into the eyes of Sophia, the All Wisdom of God, and recover a Western visionary tradition to open our hearts and imagination. In Sophia's presence, the pain and joy that arise from being fully conscious, are joined. In her serene eyes, we grasp the staff of intention and resolve to become the divinity that we are. Within the limits of our individual gifts, we become one with divine Sophia, a part of her radiant being, and create with her a conscious, loving, holy future.

WALTER R. CHRISTIE is a board-certified psychiatrist and fellow of the American Psychiatric Association. Dr. Christie also holds a master of fine arts in writing from Vermont College. He is a founder of the C.G. Jung Center in Brunswick, Maine.

Notes

1. Paul Marshall Allen. *Vladimir Soloviev: Russian Mystic.* Blauvert, New York: Steiner Books, Multimedia Publishing Corp., 1978. p. 276.

2. *Ibid.,* pp. 278.

3. *Ibid.,* pp. 273–274.

4. *Ibid.,* pp. 280–281.

5. *Vladimir Soloviev. Lectures on Divine Humanity.* Hudson, New York: Lindisfarne Press, 1995. p. 113.

6. Vladimir Soloviev. *The Crisis of Western Philosophy (Against the Positivists).* Hudson: Lindisfarne Press, 1996. p. 11.

7. Allen, p. 111.

8. *Ibid.,* p. 113.

9. *Ibid.,* p. 115.

10. Dan Merkur. *Gnosis: An Esoteric Tradition of Mystical Visions and Unions.* Albany: SUNY Press, 1993. p. ix

11. C. G. Jung. *The Archetypes and the Collective Unconscious.* Bolligen Series XX, Princeton University Press, 1980. pp. 3–53.

12. C. G. Jung. *Aion: Researches into the Phenomenology of the Self.* Bolligen Series XX, Princeton University Press, 1978. pp. 23–35.

13. Evelyn Underhill. *Mysticism: The Preeminent Study in the Nature and Development of Spiritual Consciousness.* New York: Image Books, Doubleday, 1990. p. 49.

14. Henry Corbin. *Creative Imagination in the Sufism of Ibn 'Arabi.* Bolligen Series XCI, Princeton University Press, 1969. pp. 136–175.

15. Kenneth Wright. *Vision and Separation Between Mother and Baby.* Northvale, New Jersey: Jason Aronson, Inc., 1991. pp. 11–37.

16. Diana Eck. Darsan. *Seeing the Divine Image in India.* Chambersburg, Pennsylvania: Anima Books, 1981. p. 3.

17. Fritjof Schuon. *The Eye of the Heart.* Bloomington, Indiana: World Wisdom Books, 1997. pp. 3–17.

18. Matthew Fox. *Meditations with Miester Eckhart.* Sante Fe: Bear and Co., 1983. p. 21.

19. C. G.Jung. *The Archetypes and the Collective Unconscious.* pp. 275–289.

20. Michael D. Calabria. *Florence Nightingale in Egypt and Greece.* Albany: State University of New York Press, 1997. pp. 8–11.

21. Sabina Flanagan. *Hildegard of Bingen: A Visionary Life.* New York: Routledge, 1989. pp. 4–5.

22. Robert Johnson. *Owning Your Own Shadow.* San Francisco: Harper Collins, 1991. p. 93.

23. Robert Johnson. *Lying with the Heavenly Woman: Understanding and Integrating the Feminine Archetypes in Men's Lives.* San Francisco: Harper Collins, 1994. p. 17.

24. *Ibid.,* p. 18.

25. *Ibid.,* p. 15.

26. *Ibid.,* p. 40.

27. Robert Avens. *Imagination is Reality, Western Nirvana in Jung, Hillman, Barfield, and Cassirer.* Dallas: Spring Publications, 1980. pp. 31–47.

28. Mario Betti. *The Sophia Mystery in Our Time.* London: Temple Lodge Publishing, 1994. pp. 3–28.

29. Ken Wilber. *Eye to Eye, The Quest for the New Paradigm.* Garden City: Doubleday, 1983. pp. 201–246.

J. T. HULLETT

Outside Mombasa

I STAND IN A BLACK DRESS beside the orchid-draped coffin of my father. Although the hilltop cemetery overlooks Djakarta, my superfluous thoughts slip back to Kenya and the two roads that diverge outside Mombasa. I am puzzled. World and time remove this canopied breach in the Djakarta soil from the cobbled pavement of London where my father and I began our journey, a journey upon which Kenya had been but a lay-by. Why then should images of Kenya's two roads return unbidden? Federal Road One, 400 kilometres of gently sloping grassland to Nairobi, a day-traveler's play at safari. And Highway Two—lesser traveled.

Thunder rumbles overhead. Undeterred, the vicar drones. Raindrops patter and stream from the scalloped edges of upraised umbrellas gathered beyond the tiny, sheltering canopy. The umbrellas—beneath which peek faces of various colors—form a half-circle at my back. The half-circle creates an empty, no-man's land separating me from my father's friends as if my grief were a force repelling them to some precise distance. Alone in the no-man's land, I stand head bowed, empty hands folded at my waist, idle thumbs worrying the wedding ring I still wear. John—half a world away—would not come, of course, despite the fact that the gesture could mean nothing, nothing at all.

I look toward Djakarta's vast harbour which my father called his own. A path of bent wet grass leads from the grave to waiting cars and a tiny dirt road that winds between tombstones down the hill toward the harbor and the airport from which I will now leave. Once more, Kenya intrudes with memories culled from that helter-skelter Hegira my father and I made from London after the war, that year-

Door. Paint on wood,
84×34×3½ in.,
Yoruba, Nigeria
1890–1920.
The High Museum
of Art, Atlanta, Georgia,
purchased with funds
from the Charles Belcher
Estate, 1995.192.

long odyssey during which we crisscrossed three continents, our giddy course like the paths of wind-driven embers I watched zigzag skyward after the air raid that killed my mother.

I recall Highway Two, the road that winds south from Mombasa toward Tanzania, then veers inland up the disputed Kundi range to Tsavo National Park. Of course, the mud-choked, cinder track I knew as an eight-year-old girl no longer exists. Today—as John and I discovered that last infelicitous trip to Kenya—the road is well-kept tarmac. Air-conditioned coaches deposit dry-bloused tourists at Tsavo and trundle them back to the Colonial Bar in Mombasa before nightfall the following day.

Beyond the Tsavo Reserve, however, in the wilderness past Namanga, the road remains every whit the bone-jarring trek I remember from childhood. Beyond the Reserve, Highway Two reverts to a furrow gouged across the breach between the mountains. It falters through the rift valley, then ascends in knotted switchbacks to Kisumu. The road circles Victoria warily, then careens downward across Uganda into the wet jungles of Zaire where, by and large, it exists only on a map—as a thin, red, wormlike line inching toward the continent's heart. John and I did not go that far, of course, since the road to the heart is impossible at times, even for a Land Rover—a road, sometimes yet, utterly unforgiving—a road . . . .

The vicar's hands distract me. He sprinkles water, a freakish action amid the dripping umbrellas and wind-whipped rain. Instantly, sun-drenched memories resurge like the relentless Indian Ocean waves that batter crumbling Fort Jesus in Old Mombasa.

Strange, such whims of memory—the perverse logic by which the heart plucks an instant out of time and imbues it with a world of importance. When I was eight, Kenya had seemed but a respite for my father and me on a journey whose terminus was unknown to us until we lighted in Djakarta. Djakarta rekindled my father's heart at last and became the place from which he never again departed. Establishing his business on Jalan Thamrin near Merdeka Square, he conscientiously tended accounts well into his eighty-third year—until the stroke last summer.

Djakarta is, thus, to me that Eden left behind in childhood. The ching-ching bells of the betjaks—the sweet, orchid smell and singsong chatter of the Cikini Market—the fertile essence of that place nurtures me. Djakarta, not Kenya, is the rich topsoil of my life, that layer of childhood and adolescence within which is rooted the rest. And yet—perversity of memory! — beneath the topsoil lies Highway Two like bedrock, such that—looking back as now—the moments that rise from the plain of my past like mountains, like monuments, are moments spent with my father or with John on Highway Two.

So *rich* in distractions was that road for an eight-year-old London girl whose thoughts—undistracted—exploded with images of cinderblock shelters and the wail of sirens. I relished the road's stifling heat and swollen streams—its endless toil. Long stretches of road were but muck-mired animal runs. I recall a purblind rhinoceros (enamoured of the Land Rover, I imagined) who refused us passage for more than an hour. My father flapped newspapers. He blared the klaxon and fired his Browning rifle. At gunshots the beast bolted twenty yards down the road, only to return obstinately to a horn-to-bonnet-ornament stance. By and by—ardor cooled by the Land Rover's cold heart and frigid response—the rhinoceros lumbered away, but the road was ever chockablock with such impossibilities. I remember hours when my father—gripping the recalcitrant steering wheel—uttered but grunts and curses, all attention focused through white-knuckled hands in which I vested all remaining confidence. Although my father's hands could craft a doll from a handkerchief, they nonetheless possessed an adamantine grip. My earliest memory is of those hands seizing me, defying gravity, hefting me to the aerie of his shoulders. My father's hands inspired several of my most successful sculptures. One may recall, perhaps, the black granite piece I licensed to the Jaguar Company during the seventies for advertisements—my father's hands as I remember them reining the bucking Land Rover.

Unlike my father, however, John shunned unfamiliar places, and our single trip to Kenya was made not at his suggestion, but rather as a result of my entreaties. I fancied that Africa would divert John's attention from the poor stock market that year, a turnabout that filled his mind with his stomach and his mouth with numbers—bid, ask, volume put, volume called. His litany of aches and integers—like any prayer, I suppose—signified much beyond the uttered sounds, but I heard only the droning numbers and endless requests for Maalox. Actually, the strain was long between us. At meals our silverware clinked in a lugubrious silence. I despise such silence! Much of what first attracted me to John had been his wit, his desultory conversations that played like some time-challenge chess match.

In contentious moods John argued for a more superficial base to that first attraction—his cowboy boots. Admittedly, they piqued my interest, particularly when I learned that, in a manner of speaking, John *was* a cowboy; his father owned 50,000 acres of cattle land in Wyoming where John lived until his parents' divorce. But really, does anyone ever truly fathom that inexplicable alchemy, that accidental chemistry of initial attraction? A fortuitous touch. A marble coolness in a handshake. A certain slant of light that deepens a brow or accentuates a chin. Perceptions, impressions, anticipations, and remembrance of things past, all jumbled, all rubbed together such that occasionally—ineffably—a spark is struck, an ember flares.

We met on a KLM flight from Djakarta to London. I was returning to Somerville College from a visit with my ailing father. John planned a fortnight in England after having inspected a small Indonesian concession in which his family held a percentage. He related this history while apologizing for brushing repeatedly against me. First-class legroom was insufficient for John—a lanky, Gary Cooper sort. Besides, an old wound had stiffened his leg, he said, and to ensure my belief, he hoisted his trousers-leg above his boot to reveal a ragged scar where a wild boar had gored him when he was eight. Later, I found less accessible scars which attested to the severity of the mauling, but at the time, I merely smiled and said that I, too, had been attacked by numerous bores from whom I also carried scars.

He laughed. We shook hands, spun our introductory tales, and dined the following night at Claridge's. Garrulous and innocently arrogant, John was quintessentially American. Pomp and custom ostensibly chafed, yet, covertly, he yearned for the security of tradition.

John had no numbers then. Words, laughter, stories—stories continued by post and telephone, via interludes on business trips and shared vacations, during the three weeks we spent together in Wyoming after his father died. John's younger brother retained management of the cattle ranch, while John, residing near his mother in New York City, assumed financial oversight of the family holdings. Subsequently, I myself moved to New York, where we married.

John, also, served as model for my sculptures—several acclaimed, and recent ones of lesser note. He disparaged my 'lies in stone', but once, believing himself unseen, I observed him stroke a small, unfinished carving as he might my thigh, comparing his hands of marble to those of flesh. I so startled him in his reverie that—insufferable clumsiness!—he fumbled the piece and cracked it. Seven months I had honed that stone to match my vision of what it contained.

His gaffe dated the rift that widened between us. Stories faded while numbers—this failing enterprise, that closed account—if not more strident, became more apparent. Dinners metamorphosed into solo affairs as did my annual pilgrimages to Djakarta where, upon my return, I detected signs—a disturbed lingerie drawer, a long hair on my robe, a laddered stocking of a shade I did not favour. John essayed petulant denials: Americans are so puerilely secretive with what the world takes for granted. And, frankly, the lies offended more sorely than the deeds, since the deeds—so integral a part of my own world view—could mean nothing, nothing at all.

Thus, we came to opposite sides of a breach I hoped to bridge in Africa—a place away from numbers and accounts—a place where, once more, we might be who we *were* rather than what we had become. John protested, but I prevailed. We arrived in Mombasa in early July, between the rainy seasons when the rivers run and the animals gather.

My father's old friend, Peter Mwangola, a Kenyatta clansman and mayor in those tranquil years before the Moi usurpation, insisted we stay at his waterfront villa. Morning tea on the balcony overlooked the harbor, providing a magnificent view of moldering Fort Jesus. Afternoons, I prepared fresh Indian Ocean prawns the size of small lobsters and we drank champagne and Pimm's and Momba beer beside the fresh-water swimming pool. John, conciliatory and enjoying the respite, nevertheless waxed obstinate against my plan to leave Mombasa and travel the road beyond. He pointed up the unpleasantnesses that can erupt anywhere in Africa. Offering compromise, he argued that the Park at Nairobi was a delightful place to view animals and that in Nairobi he might even conduct some business to offset the extravagance of the journey. Yielding finally to my persistence, he hired a Land Rover and outfitted us for a brief expedition south.

Outside Mombasa, Highway Two had become a dual carriageway. No dust cloud rose behind us. The air lacked its luminous, yellow quality—its bicarbonate of soda tang. At Tsavo, we found costermongers hawking souvenir Masai postal cards and Kodak film. Disgusted, I demanded we press beyond the reserve. John urged caution, but taunts goaded him onward. We plunged into the rift between Hellene and Kilimanjaro.

And—as I had hoped—in the wilderness beyond the reserve, challenged by the primitive road, estranged from taxicabs and the *Wall Street Journal,* John rediscovered that quality inside himself that once gamboled in his speech. Despite the severity of the terrain and the cramped cockpit of the Land Rover, his limp abated. We ventured afield, unearthed rare stones, witnessed sun-blotting flights of birds. From a high ridge we watched waves of grazing animals ebb and flow through the valley below. Expansive again at last, John boasted of wonders he might show me on horseback. And with his boasts returned lovemaking—that celebration of self-in-other we had lost to physical coupling and release.

Three days outside Mombasa, somewhere near Lake Natron, we camped beside a river and awoke to a pod of bathing hippopotami. Egrets chitted from the beasts' broad, glabrous backs. Tiny ears swivelled like radar dishes. '*Mu blati* the hippopotami are called there —

river pigs. Indeed, wallowing in the muddy shallows, they resembled giant, silent pigs. John lagged and urged me away from the water.

His reticence was wise. The river pigs kill more men in Africa than the lion or leopard. Unlike the often shy rhinoceros, hippos attack remorselessly upon little provocation except, perhaps, propinquity. Those lolling, lumbering islands in the brown river water can, on land, gallop much faster than a man. If attacked, one is saved but by fortune.

As I crept forward, Nikon poised, one of the behemoths galumphed from a stand of tall reeds twenty yards away. Beast and woman—equally astounded, perhaps equally intrigued—froze until John's cry shattered the spell. The river pig lowered its head and charged. Futilely—since the beast would surely catch us—John and I sprinted for the Land Rover. Just behind me, thunder boomed and shook the ground. Gasping, I reached for John's hand.

Less than an arm's length in front, John scuttled away despite his game leg. My empty hand strained. I called to his back. Thunder upon me, I stumbled and covered my head with my arms as I had learned to do as a child in the air-raid shelters where—small and helpless—jarred by an ever-forever *Boom! Boom! Boom!* outside— my father held me safe in his hands.

Abruptly, the hippopotamus veered away, having inexplicably lost interest. It slowed and waddled in a wide arc back toward the river. When it had vanished into the reeds, I lurched to my feet and scrambled to John at the open door of the Land Rover.

"I thought you loved me," I said shakily to dissipate the pressure in my chest.

John laughed nervously. "This was survival, darlin'. Love had nothing to do with it."

Unscarred and alive—now with time—we could laugh, but our excursion was spoiled. Breaking camp, John grew ever more pensive. Wrestling the steering wheel as we retreated through the wilderness to the safety of the tarmac at Tsavo, he uttered only monosyllables. I recall one time—neither of us had spoken for hours—when he blurted that the beast reminded him of the boar that had hurt him as a child. Despite my commiseration, he fell mute again.

I remember one other remark. Crossing the bridge into Old Mombasa—the green lights of crumbling Fort Jesus stark against the dark harbour—John sighed, "Guess I should've stayed where I belong."

Over the next few months—before John and I separated—the hippopotamus returned a thousand times to bedevil us.

Indeed, even while I cared for my father, the beast returned regularly in letters, resurrected of John's intractable pain. And despite my assurances that the episode meant nothing, nothing at . . .

The crowd buzzes. Umbrellas bob. The half-circle eddies and parts. Cowboy boots step into the no-man's land surrounding me. John, thinning hair rain-plastered in strands across his forehead, ducks under the canopy and squeezes my hands.

"The plane . . . the rain delayed me," he whispers. "I am so sorry. So very, very sorry."

We stand clasping hands. The vicar concludes. Nods, condolences, chatter, and the crowd returns to its affairs. John holds his ground.

"I know how much he meant to you," he says, staring at the flower-strewn coffin. Relinquishing the coffin, we walk hand in hand toward the open door of a car.

"To come all this way," I say. "I never . . . I never expected it, you know."

"Yes, I know." John says, squeezing my hand again to share unreservedly what strength he has to give.

I enter the car. John slides into the seat beside me. Jolted by the closing door, I wheel involuntarily toward the rear window to see once more the coffin. Beneath the wind-flapped canopy, two laborers have appeared and stand waiting. The car groans and pulls away.

I look again at John. The seat is cramped. He kneads his bad leg. Still pained by my gaze, he lowers his eyes.

"John," I begin, "it meant nothing! Nothing at—"

"Please," he begs. "Please, don't say it."

And he is right.

It _was_ important. _Undeniably_ important.

And he is wrong.

Because it is not the _only_ important thing. It is not the most important thing in all the world.

J. T. HULLETT is author of the Julie Harris Playwright Award-winning drama _The Pledge_. Hullett's works have also garnered a Ventana Publications Play Award, second prize in the South Carolina National Playwrights Competition, and selection as a finalist for the Heideman Award. A psychiatrist as well as author of numerous short stories, Hullett lives in southern California.

ADAM SEWARD

Rituals Stay, Symbols Follow

IT TOOK ME SEVERAL YEARS after my first sweat lodge ceremony to finally feel comfortable with wearing my traditional clothing. Not every Indian has a Certificate of Degree of Indian Blood card, and identity is primary in Indian country. One day I decided that I should forget the card for awhile and find out, in the language of my generation, what it was all about. A feather followed me along my way for over ten years, urging me to pick it up and find out who I am.

I wasn't always listening, and the feather wasn't always a symbol for me. I never dreamed that it might be, when as a teenager I listened to a musical group, Paul Revere and the Raiders, sing a song, *Birds of a Feather*. The zen-like awakening came not suddenly but gradually. Listening required waking up, and I could not find myself until I could find the center of the world. When I decided to go looking for myself, I started with a seminary course, thinking, "Well, better that than nothing." What I did not know was that the world missions course for which I signed up was an applied course. Its goal was

Painted Pastiche, Kaw, Oklahoma. Museum of the American Indian, New York, New York.

participation in a four-day field trip to South Dakota. The sponsors generously paid my way for the trip, since I was the only "skin" in the class. It was trite and laughable, when, at the end of our first day, we drove into a red-hued sunset. One of my companions wondered if we were on the "good red road."

We cannot force symbols to speak to us. They have their own timetables and speak when they wish. But they will speak. They often live in sacred places. Yet, the sacred is also everywhere: raw, controlled power flowing into all things. Rituals happen for *this* reason, in *this* time, in *this* place. A symbol can confront us anywhere. Rituals stay. Symbols travel.

WE FINALLY MADE IT TO SOUTH DAKOTA. We visited a few Jesuit fathers and a museum and then were invited to the house of a holy man where we sat and talked. He explained the symbolism of the sacred pipe, which has attached to it a feather. Then, in a casual manner, he asked us if we would like to sweat (participate in a purification ceremony). When we said yes, he gave us detailed instructions on what to do, since it was our first sweat lodge. Each of us crawled on our knees into the lodge to show our pitiableness and our relationship to the other people of Mother Earth. As each of us crawled in, we said, "Aho! Mitak' Oyasin! (To All My Relatives!)," and a strong male chorus shouted back, "Aho!" Then I scrunched up against the wall of the lodge as the helper handed in white-hot rocks on a forked stick. As we waited for the ceremony to begin, all I could think of was, "It's getting too hot . . . it's getting too hot . . *it's getting too hot!*"

A feather floats gently within my field of vision and calls me to the other world, but I can't stay in that other world. I don't know that I want to. Fortunately, I don't have to, because the Indian life of the spirit is a life lived in this world for the People. This is because Indians believe that the spiritual world and the natural world are one. The sweat lodge leader was reminding us that American Indian spiritualities are about engagement with the "natural" world. Some would call this being "grounded." Many popular works picture Indians using the natural world to "get to" the spiritual world, often to control it. This doesn't complete the circle. There is often a fascination with the otherworldly quality of Indian rituals and ceremonies. But, Indians dialogue with the spiritual world in order to survive in the natural world. One way of survival is through building relationships with spiritual powers.

All of us who went on that trip had a difficult time piecing together our relationship to those spiritual powers. I questioned how a Cherokee–Choctaw could participate in Lakota ceremonies; the others questioned how the Lakota spirits related to their Catholic patrons. I met two of my friends from the trip at a coffeehouse in Hyde Park. A few blocks from the heart of empirical reality in America, the University of Chicago, we talked about the meaning of our experiences. We knew even at that time that sagebrush was one of the sacred elements used in the pipe ceremony. I said that I'd know I was taking all of this seriously when I began to carry sagebrush around with me. One of my friends then took a matchbox from her purse. She opened it to reveal a small amount of sagebrush. We all smiled. Not long after that, she invited me to a private ceremony at a spiritual center for Native Americans. The feather had begun to help me find what I was looking for. I spent the next seven years attending pipe ceremonies, purification ceremonies, and yuwipi (healing) ceremonies. Those ceremonies told me what the world was like, and more about what it is like to be an Indian.

Symbols sometimes travel across Indian cultures and have a common reference. Although Indian cultures revere different beings, most give honor to the eagle. The Lakota believe that birds are the closest to Wakántanka, which James Walker saw as the collectivity of all the Lakota spiritual powers. The eagle flies the highest; it is only natural that it should carry our prayers to Wakántanka. Incidents associated with eagles, such as dreams or visions, are highly regarded. Yet, any feather is a reminder of Wakántanka.

One day I realized that my world had changed. I had left my apartment in Chicago to go to work. I looked down on the ground and saw a feather. I then realized that a feather was no longer a feather to me; it was a spiritual symbol. The feather continued to speak to me. One night before a pipe ceremony, the leader called my name. When I looked up, he handed me a feather, and told me to tell the people the customs of the circle. I and another person had been chosen to be speakers for the pipe circle. A year after I arrived in Boston, I gave a blackbird feather to a new friend, and by doing so gave her a part of myself. In this strange world that legislates the possession of symbols, it didn't bother me that it wasn't an eagle feather. It was a reminder of the presence of Wakántanka.

When I was leaving Chicago to go to my next stop on the "red road"—what non-Indians would call a spiritual journey—the spiritual center held a reception for me. My successor placed the feather in my hand to conduct my last prayer ceremony at the center. He then told me, "Whenever you feel sad or alone, remember the feather, and always remember who you are."

Wakántanka, unsi'mala ye. Aho mitak' oyasin!

ADAM SEWARD, a Cherokee–Choctaw, has earned master's degrees in theatre and Swedenborgian studies. He is the Swedenborgian minister in Pretty Prairie, Kansas.

JOHN L. HITCHCOCK

Mirrors of Meaning

DOROTHY PHILLIPS RAN HER FINGERS over the back of my Japanese print. "This is excellent paper," she said, "made about 1895." Because I had had enough experience feeling Persian rugs to determine their region of origin, I was not totally dumbstruck by her highly developed tactile imagery.

Of course, we all use our stored images of how different materials feel to our fingertips, but we probably haven't developed our tactile skills to such a degree as Dorothy's unless we are woodworkers, weavers, sculptors, or such. In every field of expertise, however, practitioners have spent years building specific sets of highly refined images, whether of the tones of musical instruments or the flavors present in fine wines. In order for this development to be possible, we humans must possess a powerful faculty for storing images from each of our senses. When a sensation matches the image, we *know*. Many of us have had the experience of a smell reminding us of a place we haven't visited since childhood. And here we approach an aspect of the symbolic, especially to the degree that emotions are aroused. Smells are highly efficient in arousing long lost feelings. How, though, do we recognize a smell from so many years ago? Not only is there an image of the smell, but of the accompanying emotion as well.

Imagery and feelings are both of central importance in understanding symbols, or rather in understanding the symbolic function of the psyche, for symbols are something to which we respond with our *whole being*. A symbol is not merely an idea that evokes other ideas; it grips us where we live. Whatever psychic formation actually shapes our lives is our *symbol*.

Rothehouse Kilkenny, Ireland, 1996. Photograph by S. Ripley.

*John L.
Hitchcock*

I'M ON THE ROAD, wondering whether or not I turned off the stove. Or perhaps I'm trying to remember whether I need to get more milk for tomorrow. In either case, as soon as I focus on the problem, several visual images present themselves to me, usually helpful, but perhaps not. It is quite useful, sometimes amazing, to monitor how often it is a *visual* image to which one refers when questions arise. Inwardly, I *see* something unique to this day's cooking of breakfast, perhaps the position of the frying pan, so that I'm certain that I turned off the burner as I removed the pan. Or, I get an image of the level of the milk in the container.

The visual sense gives us the prototype of an image, and I want to emphasize that all senses are imaginal. Moreover, we know a great deal about how active *visual* images are processed in the brain. There are layered *maps* with all the items in the visual field in their own relative positions. However, we are not as certain about how visual memory is stored, and we know much less about how sounds, smells, textures, and tastes are stored. We do know that stimulating the temporal lobe can induce patients to re-experience whole living scenes, at least with sights and sounds.

The best memory devices are based on visual imagery. One of the most famous memory experts of the last century said that he "placed" the items to be remembered along an imaginary path that he had worked out, and when it came time, he didn't "remember," he just "walked" inwardly along his path and "looked" to see what was there. No effort was involved. Here I am emphasizing the *givenness* of the image. Even when we are trying to remember something specific it just "comes" to us, supplied by an inner faculty that is unconscious to us.

We have images of sight, sound, smell, taste, and touch, and we have kinesthetic (interior) images of our body's position and movement as well. In psychological work, I have often asked my body to give me a position or gesture to convey a particular feeling that I am experiencing. It's a most illuminating exercise, giving me insights that I would have missed otherwise. Perhaps our more bodily senses are closer to our emotional being.

My favorite kinesthetic example is from psychological work in which a group of us were attempting to re-experience infancy. An area had been set aside as the play-floor, and we were to enter this area by crawling through a tunnel made of chairs and tables, signifying birth. As I went through, I felt a vivid rubbing on my cheeks, which I knew had to be the memory of my passage through the birth canal. It was stored in my body for half a century and released spontaneously.

I JUST OPENED MY DESK DRAWER and put my hand in without looking, to see what I could identify. There was a bottle of antacid tablets, the case of a set of lettering guides, some pairs of glasses, and a small match box, among other items. I rattled the matchbox to see whether it contained matches or thumbtacks, for I knew that I had a matchbox of thumbtacks in one of my desk drawers. My ear, and the lightness, told me that it was matches. I don't know why, but I also felt compelled to verify by *looking,* but I *knew* I had correctly identified the items. A *whole* image contains multi-sensory content, so that input from one sense stirs our knowledge of the others. That is cross-modal association. I should note that I also used my kinesthetic sense in knowing the *shapes* of the objects in my desk. It really is a sixth and separate sense.

As an aside, the senses are both differentiated and unified in the limbic system of the brain, the central area under the celebrated cerebral cortex (where we do our detailed thinking). The limbic system also contains the Papez circuit which is responsible for our emotional state. According to neurologist Richard Cytowic, we are *primarily* emotional beings, because the limbic system determines what we consider as important, and the processing done by the cortex returns there for decision and action. A pioneer researcher in this area, Wilder Penfield, even calls this region the "highest brain." It is not, however, the home of the ego, which corresponds much more closely to the cortex (the language areas and the frontal lobes), the newer layer of the brain, just as the possession of a conscious ego is very recent, perhaps only four to six thousand years old. In terms of the brain, it is this central limbic system that "gives" us the images that we need when we need them, but I don't personally believe that the brain is any more than a more or less physical component of our whole spirit-matter being.

Idea as Image

PERHAPS THE MOST POWERFUL INVENTION in all of human evolution is the *name.* Language gave birth to consciousness. It was not the first time that a sound evoked a visual image, for humans had heard animals, wind, water, storms, and such, but then the things themselves were present, if not seen. A word is something else, something that can evoke the image even when the thing or person is not present. With words, images can be manipulated and different possibilities can be imagined. Thus, words also invoke the future as idea.

But words are images, too. We all know some famous words that someone said on a momentous occasion, such as parts of Lincoln's

Gettysburg address, or Nixon's "I am not a crook," or lines from movies or television. When we hear something close to those words, whole scenes are evoked. But this also happens with "nonsense" words, as with Lewis Carroll's poem, "Jabberwocky." We speak also of the *rhythm* of speech or poetry, which evokes whole levels of human living.

With words, the question of *truth* also arises, and of *logic* as well. From learning about nature by observing, some of us have even concluded that it might be possible to *think out* the whole nature of what is. That is carrying the abstraction process to its ultimate end. My own belief is that those who follow that path have forgotten the material origins of our very ability to think, such as I have outlined above. However that may be, we do have images of words and thus of thoughts. Do we have images of *meaning?* That's where we will be heading as we go.

Our capacity to form images depends on the remnants of *external* images in our memory, whether active or deep. Even in those cases where mythological motifs unknown to the person are reproduced in fantasy, the images are built up from experience. Psychologist C.G. Jung published the case of a patient who said he saw the Sun's phallus, and that it was the source of wind or spirit. This is actually an ancient motif that was unknown to the patient. However, the patient can visualize the sun, a phallus, and wind; these are part of experience in the world. But what is it that brings them together in a meaningful *way?* It is the interior ordering or formative factor that Jung calls the "primordial image" or *archetype,* and each archetype conveys *meaningful* relationships to our conscious selves. The archetype is the wholeness of the image in its meaning for us. It is the formative representative of the source-world, or worldfield, the formless matrix of all form. Its realm is precisely that of meaning. What we experience as archetypal, we experience as meaningful. The two are practically interchangeable.

In Jung's definition, an image is something *inner,* a tendency to a certain formation, as in the term, "poetic image." It is a configuration of *meaning* which is *clothed* in such images (visual or other) as are most likely to convey that meaning to our consciousness. As with any learning, we may or may not be ready to see or receive it, which often means that we need to undergo transformation of some sort. The meaning is always there in the worldfield, ready to lead us onward to the next step.

Our experience in the world gives us the only metaphors that are at our disposal. It is hardly possible to conceive that any connections would ever be made unless the outer does indeed reflect the inner, and vice versa.

To further understand images, it is useful to try to remove the verbal component that we attach to them. You who are reading these words will also be forming mental pictures, and it is the most natural thing for us humans to move back and forth between images and words. It is always a profound experiment to stop and look around at "things" in the space where we are, and to imagine the scene without words at all. Everywhere you look, words form, "identifying" (as we would put it) the various objects, perhaps in terms of their *uses.* If you really stop to do it, it is quite remarkable. The symbol itself is the form prior to the *words.*

We are often surprised by the images that arise within us in response to a situation at hand. This is an association: "Oh, this is like that." Associations make up one of the most creative symbolic functions of the human psyche. They create the metaphors we use to communicate. But for the present, the point is that it is the common form behind the associated images that makes the metaphor. It can be clothed in many different images, and it represents something deeper and more fundamental.

Distancing

EGO-CONSCIOUSNESS is a *distancing* from things—in one sense, a *freeing* of ourselves in order to "stand back" and consider them, evaluating choices, and so forth. It is also precisely an *imaging* so that we may understand, may *see* what is there. And yet, it always remains a construct of our own, a means of grasping reality partially, at best. We grasp both the so-called inner and the so-called outer worlds solely in terms of images, and the formation of a worldview is what gives us the power to manipulate our environment and to adapt and survive in such a wide range of conditions, from deserts to the arctic, and from under the sea to walking on the moon. The price of this freedom and power is our immediacy to the worldfield, being cast from the Garden of Eden, as it were. As I noted earlier, we don't know things as they are, though clearly our images hold a certain adequacy, or our technology would be impotent.

In science, we formulate *models,* or pictures, and say that the reality is somewhat like *this.* The role of the unconscious in providing these images and metaphors from our previously acquired experience of the world, or even from mythology, is well known. This means that when we see the world, we are seeing *ourselves* in large measure.

The heart of Zen Buddhism is the spontaneous response, the pre-reflective act, pure presence in the moment. In that sense, it is correct to say that the ego gets in the way. Paradoxically, however, we can't do without our ability to reflect. Words get in the way, and yet, as T.S. Eliot put it, "I gotta use words when I talk to you." Images are interposed between our consciousness and the thing itself. We see the world as we see it, not as it is.

Another way of putting it might be to say, or see, that the essence of Zen is responding from the deep inner place from which our images are given to us when we need them, but without the ego getting in the way. That is, the ego gives its control over to the deeper parts of the self.

The artist has a greater than average contact with the inner depth, in the sense that the "inner necessity," as Kandinsky put it, is more clearly felt and can be thus brought into concrete being in a work of art. The work of art brought forth from the depths is thus a symbol of something that cannot be rationally explained. We may not produce great works of art, but we *can* be artists in living, seeking the depths within, and following our symbol. I don't believe that we need to become Zen masters in order to transcend the will of the ego and place ourselves in the service of the depths within.

In this sense, the symbol is something for the benefit of our ego-consciousness, to remind it of the ineffable depths. If we even attempt to "take inventory" of what is in the symbol we misuse it, for its function is to keep us in touch with the aliveness of the depths.

Symbols

THE WORD 'SYMBOL' HAS AT LEAST TWO DISTINCT SENSES. The first is our direct attempt to understand the visible world. We apprehend that world by means of images whose adequacy may be largely satisfactory, but never complete or perfect. Since these images are metaphors from our previous experience of the same world, something experienced as completely new is difficult to grasp.

Gradually, a new formation comes to be effective within us, but old values retain a grip on us for a long time. The world, as we understand *it*, might even be said to hypnotize us; we are *certain* that it is just what we believe it to be, especially when we have new insights. Our projections as to what it really is cannot be corrected without some sort of releasing *insight*, which usually follows a painful experience in which we are confronted with our silly pride. Every such insight is akin to awakening from a trance, yet there is no *imperative* to awaken. That depends on our boldness in risking living—risking being *wrong*.

The first sense, then, is the sense in which we never have a finally "correct" view of reality; our view is always symbolic.

The second sense, and the one with which I am most concerned, is our attempt to grasp the *numinosum*—that which we experience as holy or awe-inspiring. In other terms, it is our attempt to know God. Here, the symbol is an image which leads us to transform our lives into something more spiritual than it has previously been. I will try to indicate that the holy is present in outer experience as well as inner.

What we call *outer* is "tangible" and "material." By contrast, the *inner* is the realm of feelings, ideas, images. Matter is so convincing that it's hard to open a link with spirit, even though much of our experience links the two. Outer things *happen* to us that are meaningful to our inner being. Such events are examples of what Jung calls "synchronicity."

If you think about it, however, many outer things evoke something spiritual (symbolic) within us. The following list was merely a quick jotting of things that move us and grip us. It could be virtually infinite in length.

Horse, star, moon, rose, the sea, the sunrise, a tree, a lion, a deer. A door, threshold, window, mountain, stream or great river, a cross, stone, gold, a sword, a road. In the realm of universals: law, life, transformation, redemption, sexuality (marriage). Planting, harvest, each of the seasons, and other cycles of four. Abundance, food, birth, death. In more mythic realms: dragon, unicorn, wizard, angel, the quest. Treasure: pearl, jewel, the Holy Grail.

When a bird plumes, or does a dance, or makes a specific *call*, a pattern is fulfilled in the *other*. This is symbolic communication. Perhaps the world is dancing for us, in all that we see.

Meaning

AT SOME LEVEL, there is meaning in every association that we are given between any two events. However, that means that meaning is precisely the aim of our whole inner being, our whole inner world. Something *fits*, something seems *meant* to be the way it is. In this feeling of rightness is the root of what we call the will or mind of God. When we participate in that, we become a part of a meaningful unfolding of something. The *meantness* sometimes feels as if there is a great *plan* for the universe, but it might also just be that the universe is one in which meaning unfolds in our own human experience.

That is, perhaps meaning surrounds us at all times, but we only experience it intermittently. Alternatively, it might be that meaning is something that humans, or other highly evolved creatures, experience—an artifact or characteristic of our consciousness.

Consciousness is growing in the universe, and to be part of it, we must continually grow as well. In any case, old "answers" always eventually become stale, which means to me that something new is eternally required of us, a letting go of what we have known, and setting forth again on the path that becomes visible as we seek it.

Like love, meaning is one of the great feeling-states of humanity, and like love it is beyond definition. When it is there, however, we know it. This means that images of meaning are also part of our being, part of our innermost selves. It is something *given* to us, as the images themselves are given.

The experience of meaning, of continual transformation in all the deaths and rebirths of our lives is the only definition of salvation of which I am certain.

The fact that our consciousness is symbolic is what leaves us infinite room in which to grow. The fact that our consciousness is distanced from the Garden of Eden means that we may seek it and find satisfying images of it at all times along the way. That is real living, and the only creative use of the gift of life.

JOHN HITCHCOCK, the author of *Atoms, Snowflakes & God: The Convergence of Science and Religion* (1968) and *The Web of the Universe: Jung, the New Physics, and Human Spirituality* (1991), holds graduate degrees in clinical mental health counseling, phenomenology of science and religion, and astronomy. His third book, *Healing Our Worldview: The Unity of Science and Religion,* will be published in spring 1999 by Chrysalis Books.

PART V

Yesterday's Tracks

Spiritual Hindsight

LIKE LOOKING THROUGH A REAR-VIEW MIRROR
which reminds us
"objects in mirrors
are closer than they appear,"
our memories of past events are symbols
of present realities within us
(*much* closer than they appear!)
and can be guides to present and future actions.
Sometimes they offer the clearest guidance we have.
Other times, they provide explanations
for why we choose the paths we take.

These spiritual guideposts may appear
as natural and simple memories,
like Herzog's father and LeVan's mother,
or they may flag themselves as events
fraught with the weight
of DeCarolis' unidentified photographs
or the wings of Wright's Himalayan condor.
As Grant Schnarr notes,
"Everything in nature, in ancient stories,
legends, and mythology
reflects something within oneself."

—ROBERT H. KIRVEN

CAROL LEM

The Egg Shell

Hosing down the patio,
I find a small egg shell
cracked open and look up
to an empty nest, thinning
at the edges, its purpose
fulfilled.

But I remember how for weeks
she sat unmoved, and I'd keep
my distance, afraid of disturbing
such stillness. I forbade the gardener
from entering this sacred place.

Only once, seeing my mother
in bed, staring up, lips moving
as if in communion did I also
observe such silence. I'd wait
in the other room for her to call me.
Not a religious woman, my mother
in her last days listened to sisters and
brothers. "Ma was here," she'd say,
making circles with her finger
to describe the glow. At such moments,
my mother was doing what she must, too,
before leaving.

It's been a month
since the two little ones discovered
their wings. I'd like to know
where they go after the shell falls away.
Does space open to great space?
Or does home become another place,
close but unseen?

It's this human thing to look for signs.
Far better to go on living this life.
Still, I watch for their return,
the quiet flutterings.

CAROL LEM, born in Los Angeles, teaches creative writing and literature at East Los Angeles College. Her poems have been published in *Blue Mesa, Hawaii Pacific Review, The Illinois Review, The Lucid Stone, The Seattle Review,* and many other publications.

P.J. RUSCHMANN

The Tin Man's Goodbye

for Deb K.

I no longer move in the lanes that lovers use—
Lack of practice has rusted every word to my tongue.
No memory of lover's banter,
Sweet whispered words unspoken.
Threads that link young lovers' lives
For me have long been broken.
The words I manage
Come from a heart
Dusty from disuse—
Unpolished, often impolite,
They betray the game
But speak the truth.

And you—
Wearied by the gaps
In an education incomplete—
Are forced to fight or flee;
Stand by the rusty remnant of the man,
Or turn your back and leave....

The road to Oz is long and hard.
It promises struggle along the way:
Narrow, uphill, filled with the horrors
Of witches and curses and pain.
I wouldn't blame you if you chose
Not to follow the brick road,
Took me to task, packed your basket and ran
From heart, toward hearth and home.

P. J. Ruschmann

The terror of the journey
Holds out only the faintest hope
Like the spring-green grass of Kansas
Under a late December snow.
Of all that is yet undreamed,
Of all that could possibly be,
Of lame men leaping, the hungry feasting,
We captives, at last, set free. . . .

Yet even as you stand there
Making up your mind,
I feel my aching, nascent heart
Skip a breathless beat
And remember all too well,
What heartbreak used to be.

P. J. RUSCHMANN is a native of Grand Rapids. He graduated in 1980 from Aquinas College with a major in psychology and a minor in sociology.

ROBERT H. HERZOG

Yesterday's Tracks

"TRACKS" BY R. PAUL BOWMAN

I AM SNOWSHOEING ALONE IN MY FATHER'S woods while the others are cleaning up after breakfast and getting on with the rest of the day. No one thought father, at age ninety-one, should accompany me; not even my father.

Last summer we walked in the woods, he behind me for perhaps the first time in our lives, breaking off twigs as he went. When I asked him why, he explained, smiling, embarrassed, that the previous week he had lost his way, couldn't find the path back—lost in the woods he had first encountered in 1914 and had been walking in ever since.

I kidded him. "Why break off the twigs when, even if you find them, you won't remember why?"

Donald P. Bowman. *Tracks*. Pen, ink, and watercolor, 1983.

Now, in the snow, there is no sound of his laughter. No sound at all when I'm still, no bluejay or squirrel or chipmunk. Only the creak of the leather-binding on the ash frame of the snowshoes when I resume my walk under hemlocks, their sagging branches weighted with recent snowfall. Trees have fallen over the trails father always kept clear.

I think of framing in memory the beauty of these snowy-shouldered evergreens. And the silver beech trees holding to their pale-yellow paper-leaves when all other deciduous trees, even the oaks, are barren, save for the snow.

But I know I can never remember all this, cannot even at this moment see it all. Couldn't capture it with any camera, wide-angled lens, or with camcorder. The scope of my surroundings is around me. Although I practice Zen, I haven't meditated since coming down for the Christmas visit. Too awkward with all the people about. Now I am alone and unable to see all that is around me.

I am standing among fallen beeches sprawled across rocks three or four feet high, heightened by the drifted snow. Straight in my path, causing me to pause and consider, is a fifteen-foot hemlock. Silver slivers of snow slant through the clearing. I focus on one hemlock twig, green needles half-penetrating a snow puff. For the Zen way I breathe from my center, or "hara," exhaling my breath into the universe. I will know this twig forever. Of all the twigs in the forest, this has been seen.

The next morning I retrace the tracks—yesterday's tracks. My snowshoes sounding a counterpoint through trees themselves creaking in the rising wind. I know the spot where I stopped to meditate, for the snow is more compacted here at the hemlock starkly green against the snow. I move my shoes into yesterday's tracks and stare intently. The twig is not there.

ROBERT H. HERZOG lives in upper New York State where he teaches writing and literature at Monroe Community College. Among other projects, he is currently working on a historical narrative based on correspondence and documents kept by his grandfather, dating from the nineteenth century. DONALD P. BOWMAN, who lives in Indiana, sketched and painted the snow scene with his own father's footsteps in the woods following his father's memorial service.

PATTE LEVAN

Family Tree

I WAS SIX WHEN WE MOVED FROM CATALPA STREET in East Los Angeles to the Burbank house in a tract that had been a beanfield. No more renting. No more old-food smells coming from our walls. It was going to be a fresh start for my parents.

We moved in during a record rain in the spring of 1942. My father worked the swing-shift at Lockheed Aircraft and told my mother he was working overtime two nights a week. When she asked him why there was no extra money in his paycheck, he said it would be a bonus at the end of the year.

Aunt Edna stood with mother and me on the porch watching Uncle Ross, my father's only brother, ease a spindly magnolia tree from the backseat of his Chevy. He designed and built models in the miniature department at Fox Studio, and there was always a scent of

Joan Miró. *The Family.* Paris, May 16, 1924. Vine charcoal, white pastel, and red conté on oatmeal paper, 29¼×41 in. The Museum of Modern Art, New York, Gift of Mr. and Mrs. Jan Mitchell.

wood and resin mixed with the smell of his aftershave. He and Edna had no children. They went dancing at the Palladium on weekends.

The tree was a housewarming present. He knew that my mother longed to see a magnolia tree blooming in her front yard. I think the magnolia represented a part of some secret fantasy of hers that included a life of southern ease with a devoted, tender man.

Ross escorted her to the tree. "Here's your magnolia, Evvie." Mother seemed as touched by his remembering her wish as by the gift itself. Once planted, the tree looked scrawny and off balance, but mother was sure it would thrive if she followed the nursery instructions and gave it loving care.

Mother got sick one Saturday, and grandmother Lucy took me home for the weekend. I loved staying with Lucy. That morning we went to Westlake Park to feed the ducks, then to Santa Anita in time for the first race. The horses pounding up the dust, and the screaming crowds, felt too much like things spinning out of control. She won $20, so we went to her favorite Chinese restaurant, then stopped at Sid's Bar on the way home. Along with her bourbon and seven, she ordered a scoop of vanilla ice cream laced with port for me. The port made me sleepy, and I needed a nap when we got back.

I woke to the sound of somebody giggling in the backyard. Through the window, I could see a young woman riding around in circles on the driveway—on the dark blue tricycle I'd bought with money saved from Christmas, birthday gifts, and dimes and nickels I'd earned doing errands. She had long, thin legs, and as she pumped the pedals her knees went up and down around her ears. Her hair hung in two braids over her shoulders, and she had the biggest teeth I'd ever seen.

I ran out the back door, still in a daze, shocked that my grandmother was letting a stranger ride my new tricycle. Then I saw my father standing off to the side laughing. The girl was looking up at him, being cute, and my grandmother was sitting in the patio swing, sipping a drink. She was laughing, too. I can still feel the gut-swirl of confusion and panic that hit me like nausea beginning to peak. The too-bright late-afternoon sun was like garish Tijuana art, her plaid shirt too red against glaring white shorts, the zinnias and snapdragons around the brick patio too-brilliant in a scene that was not supposed to be happening. My father, in dress slacks, not work pants.

"Uh, this is Mickey—Mickey, this is my daughter." My father's green eyes smiled into mine, teasing and playful. "Hope you don't mind if Mickey rides your trike."

"She looks like Judy Canova," I said brightly. I'd seen her once in a movie and she'd made me laugh. I didn't know then that she was regarded as one of the homeliest women on the screen.

"Oh, she does not look like Judy Canova," my grandmother said. We waited in the silence then like actors who had forgotten their lines. Mickey hurriedly disentangled herself from my tricycle.

"Well," my father said, "We better get going." He steered Mickey toward our black Hudson, parked behind my grandmother's gray DeSoto. Two suitcases in the back seat.

"Now, you don't need to say anything to Ev about Mickey," Lucy told me after they left. "She's just a girl he works with." If mother asked me, I would have to tell her. She was fierce about telling the truth, and when she confronted me, staring at me across our kitchen table, I tried to merge with the flower pattern in the oilcloth. Then, finally, she asked the question. "Was anybody there besides you and Lucy?"

"Mickey looks like Judy Canova." I told her. It didn't make her feel any better.

I didn't see my father moving out. The next morning I woke up, and he was gone. The avocado seeds mother had been sprouting on the window sill were all over the kitchen floor, their glass jars broken, seeds split, vines already wilting in the heat of a May morning in Burbank. She swept them up later and put them in the trash. "My aim is rotten," she said. "But I landed a few." I was told he had taken a sales job in Fresno. I didn't see my father again.

Grandmother Lucy tilted forward in our green straight-backed chair that was too small for her, the wooden arms pushing into her fat. "You're not going to keep me from seeing my own granddaughter. I'll sue you. I'll say you've got men coming here."

"Get out of my house, Lucy," my mother said. She was standing in the middle of the living room looking so white and frozen she could has been dead, except that her mouth was moving.

"Get out of my house," she said. "Now."

THERE'S A SNAPSHOT of my mother standing in front of Mike Lyman's on Hollywood Boulevard in 1943. She's 36. She's taken three years off her real age to get the job at Lockheed. She weighs 105 pounds. Dark circles under her eyes. I compare it with the photograph taken when she was 23—there is still a remnant of her beauty, but the overall impression is tired. Graying early, delicate skin lined, but her posture is straight, almost defiant. The years when she stood at the ironing board in our kitchen, telling me her own dramatic version of *Alice in Wonderland,* were over. She'd taken to writing humorous poetry with a bitter edge and playing *Someone to Watch Over Me* on the piano.

The gawky magnolia tree produced one puny blossom in its third year. She cut it and brought it into the house. We breathed in the sweetness of it for days. The tree had never developed lower branches and was constantly at risk in a strong wind. Mother had tethered it to stakes, still holding out hope for its maturing into something that resembled a real tree.

The first time she went into the hospital, I stayed with my aunt and uncle and told my friends at school that mother had endometriosis and was getting a hysterectomy. It made me feel important. "Well," she told me, just before the surgery, "We don't have to worry about you ever having a younger brother." I reminded her it was an older brother I wanted. "I know," she said, "I want one too."

The Santa Anas were vicious that fall, rattling windows all night, gusting up to 60 miles an hour, tearing the laundry out of our hands before we could get it off the line and into the basket. Mother was home from the hospital, recuperating, and with instructions not to do anything more strenuous for a month than to spoon up broth.

Later that day we heard a sound like a whip snapping. Mother shouted for me as she raced through the kitchen and out the front door. The magnolia was waving wildly in the wind, one of the ropes had broken, and mother was trying to pull the tree upright and fasten the rope around the stake in the ground. "Help me," she shouted. "Get that roll of wire out of the garage. The rope's rotten."

It was nearly dark when George and Eunice pulled into their drive next door and ran over to help. Mother was still on her knees, sweating. They helped her into the house. "My gosh, kid. Why didn't you wait till we got home?" Eunice asked, "You know you shouldn't be doing that."

"There wasn't time," mother said. "But it's okay. I think we saved it." She stayed on the couch for days until the pain became so excruciating we called the doctor. She had a double hernia.

Edna had the flu, so while mother was in the hospital, I was sent to stay with the Maynards, who lived across from our old house on Catalpa Street in East L.A. Mother had kept in touch with Melba Maynard. Her daughter Elaine was my age.

Melba helped me put my suitcase and bag of books on the backseat of her old white Buick. Settling in next to Elaine made the nightmare real. I was going back to Catalpa Street, to live in the same house with Elaine Maynard for two weeks. "Have you got everything, Susie Q?" Melba never called people by their right names. Bad posture spoiled her looks; her long arms curled across the front of her body as if trying to protect all the vital spots between her neck and knees.

"You still make those little grunt noises," Elaine said, flouncing her skirt on the seat. She was referring to my habit of exhaling in short gasps when I was nervous. Elaine was, as usual, in some kind of spangled dance costume. Elaine was bright, pretty, blue-eyed,

mean, and had no talent whatsoever. Melba had been trying unsuc-
cessfully to get her into the movies ever since she won second prize
in a baby contest.

Nothing had changed at the Maynards: barely enough light to
see the dust balls under the dining room table and no comfortable
place to read. (That's because, my mother commented, they don't
read.) Melba's husband Rudy was a big, silent man who walked
around with a tentative, puzzled expression, like somebody on the
verge of discovering he's in the wrong house.

I'd endured three days there when after dinner I was on my knees
looking under the couch for my Nancy Drew book, and my rear in
the air must have been too tempting for Elaine. She delivered a swift
little kick to the target, but her shoe tap hit my tailbone, the pain shot
through my back as I whirled around and threw my whole weight on
her. I pounded her head on the floor, pulling her hair and beating her
face with my fists. She screamed in terror. I was frightened of my
rage, but I couldn't stop. Melba began shrieking and pulled me off.
Elaine's nose was bleeding down the little gauzy outfit she was trying on for her recital. They all look at me as if I was some sort of
crazed monster.

I was ostracized. The family avoided contact with me. Elaine refused to go to her recital because of her swollen nose. I was delivered
to school and left to my own devices.

On Saturday, Melba took me to the hospital. A smallish, waxy
looking man in a black suit was also visiting my mother. He had
brought her flowers. I was told he was Alfred, Melba's unmarried
brother. Toward the end of the visit, Alfred and Melba left the room,
and I could tell my mother everything that had happened. She
looked smaller and more tired than ever.

"We wouldn't be here," she said, "if it weren't for that damned
tree. Aunt Edna's feeling better now. You can spend the rest of the
time with them."

Uncle Ross had rebuilt a 1914 Ford and joined the Horseless
Carriage Club. On a trial run, he drove me by the house the day
mother was due to come home. Top down, wind tearing at us, we
rolled up to the front yard to find one of the moorings had come
loose and the magnolia tree cracked in half at the waist. Its sparse fo-
liage and upper body were sprawled on the grass like some top-heavy
actress who had attempted a bow and fallen into the orchestra pit. I
thought about how I might glue the tree back together, just until my
mother got well. Uncle Ross just shook his head and drove us over to
Hollywood Boulevard where we cruised up and down waving to people until it was time to collect mother from the hospital. Nobody
mentioned the tree.

She laughed when she saw the tree the next morning, her arms wrapped around her stomach to keep from hurting. She looked out the window at it for a long time.

It stayed that way for weeks. She would walk past it several times a day without even glancing at it. Finally I put the dead part out by the incinerator.

The war was over. The men were returning to their jobs, and the women were being returned to their kitchens. Mother had barely begun paying her hospital bills when they laid her off at Lockheed. The day she lost her job, she came home early and changed into her gardening slacks. She got the hatchet and limb saw from the garage and began chopping at the trunk of the tree, then sawed it off even with the ground.

Alfred was dating mother, arriving in a faded tan Studebaker every Saturday evening. Dinner and a movie. Sometimes I was invited. Their conversation had long pauses. Mother and I wanted to talk about the movie. Alfred didn't.

Mother had been training as a grocery checkout clerk, but they had her marking prices for two weeks instead of learning the cash register. When they found somebody younger and faster, they laid her off and docked three days' pay for the training she never had. "My back is to the wall," she explained after she'd agreed to marry Alfred. There's a photograph of us on their wedding day, standing with the Maynards in front of the three-foot square of earth where the magnolia had been.

"You and I are going to be cousins," Elaine said, looking at me like an over-friendly puppy. We were on the front porch stuffing down wedding cake. She scratched at scabs on her knees and elbows. I hadn't seen her since the episode. She never used to have scabs, and if she had, she wouldn't have picked at them. She told me she found my Nancy Drew after I left, read it, and got the next two books in the series. She then asked if I'd like to borrow them. It took me a while to piece it together.

After that day when Elaine couldn't go to her recital, she managed to fall and cut her chin just before her next program. When another show was scheduled, she fell down and skinned both knees and elbow for good measure.

"Mama stopped the lessons, and I don't have to do any more shows," she whispered. "She says I'm getting so clumsy. She's looking for a new ballet teacher." She sighed.

"You mean you didn't want to be in the shows?"

"No," she said. "I hate it."

I slowly grasped that in beating her up I had, it seemed, liberated her. And instead of hating me, she was grateful. Apparently I'd inspired her to maim herself so she could stay off the stage and get some control of her life. She turned out to be a pretty nice person when she wasn't being tortured into a bad replica of Shirley Temple. But I didn't see much of Elaine after we turned eleven. Years later, when I heard she had gotten a scholarship to the University of Redlands, I hoped Melba had forgiven her for not becoming a movie star.

The marriage lasted a year, a very long year. The strange arguments would often begin at the dinner table and last for hours after I'd gone to bed. Alfred would seize on some incident and insist that my mother or I had done it just to hurt him. He also thought we should spend Sundays visiting one or another of his many relatives. There were interminable conversations carried on in drab living rooms among people who had nothing to say to each other. The only fun was visiting the Maynards.

During that year, mother planted asters in the bare spot where the magnolia had been. She was slowly getting her strength back and gaining a little weight, despite the late-night harangues. "I think your brother has a persecution complex," my mother told Melba. "I can't stand much more."

"Well, Muffin, I told you before I introduced him to you that he's a little peculiar," Melba said.

"He's beyond peculiar," my mother said. "He's just short of crazy."

I think the last straw was when he announced one night that Irving Berlin was a better composer than Gershwin. "You're entitled to like Irving Berlin better than Gershwin," she said, "but that doesn't make him a better composer."

"No," Alfred said. "Irving Berlin is the better composer, and you know it. You just argue about these things to hurt my feelings."

He left soon afterward. Again, I don't remember the actual departure. One day he was just gone.

Most of the yard chores had been turned over to me, and when I went out one Saturday morning to deadhead the asters, I discovered something with glossy leaves growing up in the middle of the flower bed. We paid no attention to it until it had grown up past the asters.

"Those are just suckers," a neighbor told us. "It won't amount to anything."

They weren't suckers. The thing kept growing, in sturdy, straight, perfect symmetry, putting out leaves and branches every few days. The magnolia tree was making a spectacular comeback.

Things got better after that. A woman, also a divorced parent, helped mother get bookkeeper training, and she got a decent-paying job. During the next ten years, she developed close friendships with a group of single women who went on trips together and held potluck parties to celebrate the milestones in their lives. Most of them were still hoping the right man would come along, but they had learned they could have some pretty great times with each other.

When mother heard somehow that Grandma Lucy's husband of only a few years had committed suicide, she said, "It was probably self-defense. But it's wrong of me to deprive you of your grandmother."

It must have taken a lot for mother to call Lucy. But they had their reconciliation. As my grandmother was leaving after dinner she said, "Ev, I never meant you any harm. I always thought the world of you."

My mother looked at her for a long time before she answered. "Lucy, I believe you did."

The magnolia continued its miracle, growing into the tall, well-balanced beauty it was meant to be. Mother would stop and sniff the blossoms occasionally, shutting her eyes and drinking in the heady scent. But she didn't want them in the house. "They're too sweet," she said.

PATTE LEVAN, editor of the monthly Swedenborgian publication *The Messenger,* holds a bachelor of arts degree from Antioch University. She is the author of a number of published works, including two novels, a history of Parents Anonymous, and several booklets for the National Committee for Prevention of Child Abuse. She first appeared in the Chrysalis Reader *The Power of Play* (1996) with "Follow the Man on Las Palmas."

Claims

NOTHING ELSE CAN DRAW YOU LIKE A SHOP WINDOW. Think of it as a barrier of glass which you, on the outside, experience as longing. Isn't that, after all, what glass really is, a transparent sort of longing? Step inside, tell the clerk what you want to see, to hold, and the feeling will soon fade as the object is in your hands. You may still buy it, but you'll never buy what it was that drew you to it, that held you there with the glass between you and it.

Years ago there was a pawn shop in a city I passed through from time to time. This was in the days when main streets were nicer places to walk, the days when restaurants had real names and real food, and drugstores had ice-cream counters with revolving stools, drugstores where the pharmacist owned the business and you had to go up to the back and speak discreetly if you wanted to buy something personal.

One afternoon I paused before the window of that same pawn shop and let my eyes wander over the merchandise on display. I was single and traveled for an insurance company. Collisions, fires, boats on the rocks, in those days we'd cover it all. The window held me as much as did what it kept me from. I wasn't fond of pistols; there were plenty of those, naturally, from big cowboy revolvers and semi-autos to sleazy little chromed pieces with ivory grips–"something for the ladies" said the card set among them. I reviewed the watches, passed over a small sea of rings, several tiers of steins with bas-relief faces and hinged lids, ignored the hand-cuffs, the nightsticks, and settled, finally, on a collection of cameras, a few of which looked worth owning.

Polaroids hadn't caught on yet. People were still patient, still understood how to wait. A Rollieflex caught my eye. I went in to have a closer look. The man behind the counter was seriously obese but covered it by wearing expensive pants, properly cut, and a silk shirt

without a wrinkle. He sported a pencil-thin moustache and moved briskly, which seemed to lighten him even more. I thought of Ronald Coleman with a thyroid condition or, maybe, Don Ameche.

"You won't find a more reliable camera than this one," he said, lifting the Rollieflex from its perch in the window. His voice was softer than I expected and somehow fit his clothes. "You must be a professional, I mean if you want something like this."

"Who says I want it," I told him.

"A lot of guys would," he countered. "I've been back and forth with it a dozen times this week alone."

"Then something has to be wrong," I suggested, "since it's still here."

"Nothin's wrong," he said testily.

"There's still film in it," I observed.

"Darndest thing," he remarked, easing off as much as I had. "I only noticed after it'd been here a while. But it's only six shots along, so I figured I'd leave it there and let whoever bought it finish the roll." I checked the ASA dial to find the speed and then guessed from that what kind of film it was.

"It ain't color," he said, "I know that much."

"Six gone, six to go . . ." I mused.

"Film's free." He tried a smile.

"How can I resist," I said and bought the thing.

THE DARK ELEGANCE OF A REALLY GOOD CAMERA makes it seem somehow alive, this one all the more so because there were images inside, latent but there. There were six shots left. I used them that very day and wrote off the cost of the camera in doing so. The seventh and eighth went to collisions, no injuries in either case, but the claims were still hefty because one was a 'Vette, the other a Caddy. I used the ninth and tenth at a burger place. The wooden floor under the grill had caught fire. No foul play as far as I could see. Even with a tin plate underneath, the floorboards still dry out. Over the years the kindling point drops lower and lower. There was no serious damage except where the grill fell through to the basement. The appliance was a total loss, but again no injuries. I used my Speed Graphic to take the basement shot because it was too dark to get anything down there without a flash.

As for the twelfth picture, on the way back to the office I took the shore road and drove out to a point of land overlooking the ocean. There was a little parking place with a few picnic tables, a green barrel, even one of those coin-operated binocular scopes for viewing the old lighthouse and ledges that it once marked. By then it was almost

Helen Lundeberg. *Double Portrait of the Artist in Time.* Oil on fiberboard, 47¾×40 in., 1935. National Museum of American Art, Smithsonian Institution, Washington, D.C., Museum Purchase.

three-thirty. I had the whole place to myself, so I decided to waste a little time, enjoy the view, whatever, and then check in before going home. Call it a once-in-a-lifetime thing, but as I raised the Rolleiflex to use up the final frame (a seascape was what I had in mind) something big and silver which did not in any sense resemble an airplane came hurtling toward the point and then without slowing down, managed a ninety-degree turn to my left and swiftly climbed. I wanted to watch it go, but I wanted also to take a picture, so I set the focus at infinity, aimed as best I could and clicked the shutter before it went out of sight. Then I rewound the roll and returned to the car, wondering all the time if I'd actually seen a flying saucer. I'd once read of a man in California who'd taken some shots of a saucer-like object out over Mount Palomar. That was in 1952, but I didn't believe a word of it. The pictures I saw in the magazine proved nothing as far as I was concerned. He could have tossed something into the air and photographed it on the way down. But no one had tossed what I saw. If only the camera could prove it! I turned back before getting into the car, almost believing that if I looked hard enough, I'd see it again.

BACK AT THE OFFICE, I turned in my paperwork and picked up names and addresses for the following day. All I wanted to do now was rush home and develop the film. In spite of my excitement over the final picture, my fascination with the first six had not diminished. Within an hour I was groping in my darkroom, really a converted pantry, feeding the film into a development can. A few minutes later, in the red of the safelight, I hung the film up to dry. To my deep satisfaction, there was an image in every frame. I went out to the kitchen, fixed a sandwich and ate while I waited. When the roll was dry, I snipped it into twelve squares, set the claim shots aside and made a contact print of what remained.

I'VE KEPT THEM TO THIS DAY because, in their own way, they've taught me that the world is more than what it seems. First, there is the flying saucer. The picture shows it, impossibly there, silver and majestic against the sky. I tried to convince the newspaper. They suggested a tabloid. I showed it to a friend at work who believed me but told me no one else would. The first part was a lie, the second part, sober advice; and I took it. Even so, I saw what I saw. Nothing will ever change that.

As for the other six frames, they turned out to be pictures of an unknown girl's first Communion. I know this because, though I am not Catholic, several of the people I work with are; and they con-

firmed my guess. The child's face is angelic in its innocence and perfectly featured. In four of the shots, she wears white gloves, carries a
small bouquet and prayer book. In the first, she is on the church steps
with her mother. I say this because there is a definite resemblance between them. The mother is almost beautiful. I can't identify the
church, nor is anything familiar in the scene. According to the date
imprinted on the film, the event had taken place less than two years
before. That saddened me because something unfortunate must
have happened. Had someone stolen the camera and pawned it in
another town? Is there some other explanation? I'll never know. In
the second, the holy child is with a man in a light-colored suit, her
father I suppose. He is kneeling on her left. In the third, she is with
them both. The fourth shows her with a priest who looks like Spencer
Tracy in clerical garb. Five and six are different. This same child is at
the seashore. In five she is standing beside a sandcastle, which I suppose she has just finished building. Her pride and delight are un-
mistakable. In the sixth, my favorite, her father is buried up to his
neck in the sand. There's a slightly demonic look on her face. I don't
know what she had in mind, but in no way does it displace that celestial sweetness more apparent in her Communion scenes. I suppose her mother took the last one.

If only I could have found them. By now she's probably a mother herself. I have often wondered if the beach above which the flying
saucer broke into my universe is not the same as that in pictures five
and six. Often, too, I have wondered what "Father Tracy" would have
thought had he been next to *me* that afternoon, or would the glass
through which he saw the world not have permitted such a transla-
tion of the light? I'll never know. Only the pictures remain, and they
raise more questions than they could ever answer. That's how it always is when I get them out and hold them to the light.

VINCENT DECAROLIS is primarily a writer of fiction but has many scholarly
interests, which include the pre-Socratics, William Blake, the works of C. G.
Jung, Emanuel Swedenborg, and New Testament studies. He lives in
Freeport, Maine.

GRANT R. SCHNARR

Sun Tzu and the Art of Spiritual Warfare

A KEY CONCEPT THAT ORIGINALLY ATTRACTED ME to certain spiritual teachings is the idea that everything in nature, in ancient stories, legends, and mythology reflects something within oneself. This understanding has enriched and, in fact, broadened my work as a Swedenborgian minister. Swedenborg's explanation of the Book of Exodus, for example, helped me to understand how a nation's struggle to flee slavery and to find a promised land was a metaphor for my own struggle to escape the slavery of an addiction and a compulsive nature and to move toward spiritual freedom and happiness.

Not long ago I came across a popular ancient work that, at first, seemed quite unrelated to spiritual teachings. The title jumped out at me: *The Art of War.* The book was written in ancient times by a Chinese warrior–philosopher, Sun Tzu. I remember leafing through the book in a friend's home, looking through the index and chapter headings. I don't really understand why, because I am not especially interested in war or in tactics about how to overcome an adversary. But the more I read, the more involved I became. I asked my friend if he were familiar with the book, and he said, "It's really not my cup of tea. Take it with you." I was somehow unknowingly delighted.

Upon returning home I began to study Sun Tzu, who takes the reader through the strategies of different kinds of warfare, when to

fight and not to fight, how to assess the enemy's strengths and weaknesses, how to win without fighting at all. Immediately I found help in dealing with conflict and adversarial relationships, whether with opponents across a boardroom or on the racquetball court. It was all in fun, but seemed to give me an edge in adversarial situations. Sun Tzu says, for instance, "The army that takes the field first, well rested, will gain the victory." So I'd start showing up early for my weekly racquetball war with my good friend David. When he came jogging onto the court, still processing his last business meeting, weakened by his struggle through the traffic to make his appointment on our field of battle, and only barely able to do two or three stretches

Performing Horse with Rider. Earthernware, 23 in., Chinese, Tang Dynasty, eighth century. The Saint Louis Art Museum, Museum Purchase.

before beginning the game, there I stood poised for battle, well warmed up, centered, strategy in mind, rested in body. My winning percentage skyrocketed.

But learning how to gain the upper hand over a fellow human left me feeling a bit guilty. Learning how to battle others effectively was not exactly my own cup of tea, but I realized that my growing excitement about the warrior–philosopher's message was not so much based upon literal application as upon its spiritually symbolic significance. The work is based on the Taoist philosophy that one must not simply react to external circumstances, but act into them with purpose, awareness, and centeredness. Those familiar with Taoism know that it holds peace as a high ideal. Interestingly enough, *The Art of War* is not an exception to this. Its goal is to teach how to win without fighting at all, to conquer an enemy by understanding the enemy, the self, the circumstances, and to maneuver in such a way on the battlefield that actual conflict may be avoided, and if not, the battle will be swift with minimal bloodshed. It is about outsmarting your adversary and staying out of areas of weakness and potential trouble.

When I began to see that this strategy could be used as a metaphor for combating inward foes, Sun Tzu's words were suddenly transformed into an illuminating guide. Bringing together Sun Tzu's battle strategy and Swedenborg's science of symbolism, I found a spiritual companion and mentor guiding me through the perilous terrain of my world within. The enemies that Sun Tzu and Swedenborg helped me to understand, to outwit, to subdue, were my own personal demons.

Battling inner demons is nothing new. The struggle between the base animalistic shadow-self and the noble, spiritual being within is something everyone experiences on various levels at various times. Revelations have been written about this struggle between light and darkness, between good and evil. With Swedenborg's symbols and Sun Tzu's strategy, I found myself better able to deal with my spiritual enemies on a daily basis, knowing how to avoid their attacks, how to strive for the quick victory, and even how to rise again after defeat.

SUN TZU BEGINS BY SAYING, "Warfare is a vital matter of the nation. It is the ground on which life or death is determined and the road that leads to either survival or ruin. Therefore it must be examined with the greatest care."[1] This is certainly even more true with the spiritual warfare each of us faces against the personal demons, destructive impulses, and forces of darkness that battle to destroy us. It is vital to our human condition and the ground upon which our spiritual lives struggle for survival. Swedenborg points this out by saying,

> Let it be known that no one can be reborn without temptation, and that each person suffers very many temptations, following one after another. The reason for this is that rebirth takes place to the end that the life of the old person may die and a new, heavenly life may be introduced. From this one may recognize that [spiritual] combat is altogether inevitable; for the life of the old person stands its ground and refuses to be snuffed out, and the life of the new person cannot enter except where the life of the old has been snuffed out. From this it is clear that fierce combat takes place between mutually hostile sides, since each is fighting for its life.[2]

For me, the idea that the most important issue in my life is to conquer my own destructive inclinations actually brings me comfort. Instead of wondering, "Why is all this conflict happening inside of me? Is something wrong?" I know that this is part of the growth process. Though I feel pain from conflicting desires within me, I know that if I persevere I can come into greater and more perceptible states of real inner peace, and with that peace I experience a new freedom from dysfunctional compulsions and destructive tendencies. I can receive and bask in joy, having taken new territory away from my spiritual enemies within and established solid ground on spiritual principles and love. This combat is vital to my own spiritual condition. It is the ground upon which my own life is determined. Sun Tzu says,

If you know the enemy and yourself
You will never be at risk in a hundred battles;
If you do not know the enemy but know yourself
You will sometimes win and sometimes lose;
If you know neither the enemy nor yourself
You will be at risk in every battle.[3]

Self-awareness is an important component in eastern philosophy, as it is in the teachings of Swedenborg, who urges the reader to examine oneself, discover the destructive aspects, pray to God to help combat and remove them, and to begin a new life. What Sun Tzu helps point out is how important it is to know not only my inner enemy, but my strengths and weaknesses in dealing with that enemy.

One of my spiritual enemies is fear. It is real and it can be paralyzing in my life. Exploring what may have given rise to this fear in my past, as well as what may give it presence in the future, are all means of knowing the enemy. For instance, since I was very young I have experienced a heightened fear of dying when I travel to distant places. Before taking on the discipline of examining myself and my spiritual enemies, I would simply tough it out when I traveled. Not knowing why I experienced a heightened sense of danger far beyond what one might call the normal anxieties associated with travel, I found it a baffling mystery. Later, through applying the principles of self-examination, and building an awareness of myself and my spiritual enemy of fear, I discovered that this fear stemmed back to childhood. My mother had lost her first son, my only brother, to a sudden illness. I realized that my fear had its roots in my mother's fear for my safety. Through vigorous self-examination I realized that I had grown up sensing this fear and coming to the unconscious conclusion that I should be scared when I leave the comfort of home, and that there was a good chance I might die. I also realized later on that I had an unconscious contract with my mother that I wasn't allowed to die. I was too important. I know this sounds awfully Freudian, and it is, but this type of self-awareness helped me to see the fear and let go of those aspects that didn't belong to me. I didn't have to carry my mother's fear anymore. But if I do not also reflect on how and when I am placing myself in a state of mind which enables and perhaps even nurtures that fear, I have a hard time dealing with it. If I can explore what it is within me that ushers that fear into my life, and the unconscious payoff I receive from allowing it to march onto the fields of my conscious life, I can develop a sound strategy to defeat it. From this understanding, I can make a choice whether I will combat it, outmaneuver it, or simply run away. It gives me the upper hand.

My worst scenario is a surprise attack by a destructive tendency, a quick loss in battle. I wouldn't know why it happened, or what caused it. In an argument, for example, rage can surface suddenly, causing great damage to a relationship. The person unaware of self or the enemy is surprised by his or her anger, doesn't have a clue where it came from, nor how to deal with it in the future. This is true with any destructive tendency, be it lust, self-pity, addiction. If I am ignorant of myself and my spiritual enemies, I walk blindly through the spiritual battlefields, defenseless against enemies who attack at will. Part of the discipline in this battle for spiritual growth is to know your inward enemies well, to know your self even better, and to act wisely in battle strategy to defeat those enemies in order to grow spiritually.

The following is one lesson that I find invaluable. It is Sun Tzu's advice: "The expert in battle takes his stand on ground that is unassailable, and does not miss his chance to defeat his enemy. For this reason, the victorious army only enters the battle after having first won the victory, while the defeated army only seeks victory after having first entered the fray."[4] To stay out of places and circumstances that may cause trouble is good advice but not always followed. I struggle with certain temptations or desires, but don't stop to think if I can change the outward circumstances to give myself the upper hand. If an alcoholic is struggling with addiction, going to a bar to meet friends is not a good start. To be unassailable to that particular enemy means no more bar scenes. People who struggle with lust and adultery have only to stop sharing a cup of coffee with that attractive colleague. It is easier to win without fighting than to tough it out in battle. A young adult caught in the conflict of peer pressure to break the law and her own sense of right and wrong, may decide that the battle is too dangerous to fight on the familiar terrain of old friendships. It is better to leave potentially dangerous friendships behind, if peer pressure is leading against the law, until she has the strength to deal with the peer pressure in a constructive way.

The practical advice of maneuvering onto ground which is unassailable to the inward enemy may seem simple, but it is incredibly effective. This is how a spiritual combatant can enter into battle after having first won the victory, or even win the victory without going into battle at all!

There are many other lessons from Sun Tzu: how to throw your entire force behind you in conflict, lessons on staying close to your source of supplies, on different kinds of attitudes in battle, different kinds of terrain, different kinds of enemies. Through Swedenborg's insights about spiritual combat and symbolism, much can be learned on a very practical level about how to deal with one's spiritual foes, how to gain victory over the lower self, and move in freedom toward happiness and inner peace. In the end the spirit born of battle grows to be mature and refined, growing in ageless wisdom, yet capturing and maintaining youthful zeal. When it moves swiftly, it is like the wind. When it proceeds slowly and majestically, it is like the forest. It is as fierce as fire against inward foes and as immovable as a mountain. It is as unpredictable as a shadow. Its action is like lightning and thunder.

GRANT R. SCHNARR is the author of several books. He graduated from the Academy of the New Church with a master's degree in 1983.

Notes

1. Sun Tzu. *The Art of War.* Jon Jin, trans. Chapter One.
2. Emanuel Swedenborg. *Arcana Caelestia.* Vol. 1, Paragraph 8403.
3. Sun Tzu, Chapter Two.
4. *Ibid.,* Chapter Four.

LANI WRIGHT

Some Kind of Sign

Kano Yosetsu. *Hanging Scroll.* Ink and colors on paper, 47×44.3 cm. sixteenth century, Muromachi, Momoyama Period. Asian Art Museum of San Francisco, The Avery Brundage Collection, San Francisco, Gift of Mr. and Mrs. Walter Shorenstein (B76D6).

IN 1991 WHILE MY MOTHER WAS SLOWLY DYING, I went to Nepal to lose myself in the mountains and hopefully to find myself there, too. I went because when your life is full of the pain of someone's dying, it gives an urgency to all the things you've always wanted to do and haven't. Losing my mother (to a debilitating stroke) whom I had always counted on brought me to a place with no borders or boundaries—a place I'd never been, without signposts, solid ground or protocol. In this place I was tossed back and forth between being a child and being Nurse Ratchett—remember her from *One Flew Over The Cuckoo's Nest?*—in charge of the loony bin that my mother's life and, by extension, my own had become.

This made it easier somehow to go off and travel into new territory. I was at sea in my "normal" life; maybe I'd find safe harbor in the exotic East. I decided to go for a long trek, keeping my eyes open until I found something significant. What that might be I wasn't sure. But I expected there would be some kind of sign. A polestar perhaps. Something to indicate that I would not only survive, but maybe even learn a thing or two.

The particular walk I chose followed the thin line of a milky river toward the Tibetan border. For nine days the predominant direction was up. The oxygen thinned. The air cooled. Green fields of rice gave way to golden fields of barley and eventually to fields of dirt grazed by goats and sheep until every last stalk and root had been devoured.

The landscape looked like a long, narrow Chinese painting—the kind that hangs between scrolls and features tumble-down mountains sliced by a deep river valley with medieval flat-roofed villages clinging to the mountainsides.

Because the air was so clear and the days so sunny, everything in the landscape stood out in sharp relief. This made even the most ordinary rock in the path seem imbued with magical qualities. Or maybe that's how it is when you are so far from home, doing something you've always dreamed you might do.

On the ninth day I entered the Manang valley and came to the village of Bragga. I spent that afternoon sitting on a bench watching the villagers around me as they did their work. Later, I took a walk through town and lost my balance coming down a sandy path. I fell, creating a racket of rattling stones as I slid down the slope out of control.

An old Tibetan woman, with the face of a cherub, came out of a near doorway to brush me off. "Chai?" she kept saying over and over. Finally, it dawned on me she was asking if I wanted tea.

I followed her up a ladder, carved out of a single log that looked to be 400 years old or older—maybe even from the time of Jesus. I climbed behind her up to the second floor and stepped off the ladder onto a flat terrace. Baskets of drying things stood all around. She didn't pause but led the way into the house. It was dark with walls of thick layered stone. I sat on the smoothed mud and played with her kittens while she made the tea. She took the water from a thermos, and suddenly the thought flashed through my mind unbidden— maybe she hadn't boiled the water well enough. Would I get sick if I drank her tea? At the same time I was so charmed by her sweetness and her kittens, and by being in my first Tibetan kitchen, that I threw caution to the wind and just drank it. Afterwards, when I didn't get sick, I laughed at myself. It was the first time I had done something so foolish since my mother had started her dying. It felt so good, I cried.

The next day I climbed the cliffs behind the town to see if I could find a small monastery that was said to be in the area. It was a day as clear as hindsight. I startled a flock of snow pigeons up from their roosts and stood a long time in one place watching them circle overhead—their bellies gleaming white against the blue sky as they wheeled and came around as one body in perfect unison. I climbed another hour up the shaky little goat-track path listening to my heart pounding. From the top, the entire Annapurna range spread out in a line spilling over with blue rivers of ice.

I walked in the direction I thought the monastery might be for another hour or two, but I never found it. I didn't mind. The trip had already started to feel like a pilgrimage, and as any pilgrim can tell you, a pilgrimage is more about what you discover along the way, than it is about where you end up.

I sat cross-legged on the edge of the cliff where I could gaze over the valley to the snow-capped peaks on the other side. Way down below me, about the size of a dime, I could see the yellow tent where I would sleep that night, and tiny human beings going about their business. I closed my eyes and listened to the silence echoing across the valley.

It was then I felt a breath of cold air against the back of my neck and heard the great whoosh of air through wings that surely must have been angel size. I opened my eyes in time to see a bird glide a few feet over my head with wings as wide as I was tall. I had never seen a bird this big or this close before. A lammergeier! The Himalayan version of the American condor. I had just enough time to note its sizable talons, and then it was gone, soaring into the thermals, leaving me feeling as if I'd just been buzzed by a jet.

It was only then I had time to be scared, time to think that if it had decided to pick me up in those claws and carry me off over the valley, I would have had little choice in the matter. I pictured falling that great distance to the valley floor and dying there the size of an ant in the vast landscape.

I cried out, not in anguish, but for joy at the sweet sense of release this momentary imagining had sent flooding through me. My eyes blurred with tears, and at the same time I could see clearly for the first time that in the end my mother's death would turn out to be, after all, the natural order of things.

LANI WRIGHT has been an outdoor educator, language teacher, and college administrator. Her voice has been heard reading commentary on women, nature, and spirituality on the National Public Radio station WFCR in Amherst, Massachusetts. She lives and writes in southern Vermont.

PART VI

Follow the Pleiades

The Mainstream

IF WE SEE THE SYMBOLS THROUGH,
seeing through symbols is like
reading a book all the way through:
we reach a conclusion.
It may be satisfying or clarifying,
or it may point a new direction
for further exploration.

Seeing through symbols
lets us see farther ahead or further inward
than we can see with our physical eyes,
turn ecstatic dancing into a sense of the meaning of being,
make coherent sense of disparate objects in a dream,
or give cosmic significance
to ponderosa saplings in a wheelbarrow.
It can help us relate humanity and divinity
in the washing of an invalid body
and give meaning to a daring and soaring search
for something
that even the sharpest of physical eyes can never detect.

—ROBERT H. KIRVEN

PAUL FINN

Inishmaan

Follow the Pleiades. Daybreak.
The red earth between us
bulls and horses with sudden tongues
open-mouthed fishes speaking and
another name written on the yellow envelope.
I will show you across the plain
toward the coast. Here beneath an olive tree
he saw the glimmering fire, the sky and earth
the constellation communicating secrets.
A story about necessity. A knot.

PAUL FINN lives in Glasgow, with the painter Irene MacNeil. His poems have
appeared in *Shenandoah, Santa Monica Review, The Florida Review, The
Malahat Review, Paris Atlantic, Puckerbrush Review,* and *Puerto del Sol.*

ROBERT BLY AND SUNIL DUTTA,
TRANSLATORS

When the Sky Clears

The drop grows happy by losing itself in the river.
A pain when beyond human range becomes something else.

One man's heart died when he insisted
    on treating his own problems.
Sometimes people solve jute-knots by rubbing them on rocks.

Since I am weak, I sigh instead of weeping.
My experience tells me that water can change and become air.

The sky abruptly clears following thick clouds and heavy rain.
The clouds, recognizing separation, cried and vanished
    into non-existence.

We make the back of the mirror green in order to see our faces.
Sometimes nature makes the front of the mirror green as well.

We love seeing the beauty of poppies and lilies.
When the eyes lose themselves in the colors,
    they are seeing at last.

—GHALIB

ROBERT BLY is a winner of the National Book Award and the author of numerous collections of poetry. His lively translations of such poets as Rumi
and Ghalib have brought the moral force of other worldviews to the main-
stream of modern life. This poem is translated from the Urdu.

The Dance

Dancing Celestial Figure (apsaras). Bronze, 39.3 cm., Cambodia, eleventh century. Museum of Fine Arts, Boston, Gift of Denman Waldo Ross.

EVERYTHING I HAVE LOVED IN MY LIFE distills into a single face, into one bead of sweat traveling down her temple, over the silky black hairs at the side of her head, where the pulsing of my guru's heart is visible—that one salty drop generated by the heat of her dancing, ecstatic body. Gurumayi danced for the love of her guru, Baba Muktanandya, her body a porous cup filling and filling, spilling into the meditation hall, spilling onto everyone in it, onto me. It was the night of her birthday, the culmination of an all-day celebration at her ashram in the Catskill Mountains.

The morning after, I would lift my head from my pillow and look over the side of the bunk bed, down to my beloved friend Mary, whose head was still on her pillow. Her blue eyes were open, stunned, her white hair around her lovely old face. I would say sleepily to her, *Was it all a dream?* Her eyes the color of sky would tear, would spill, her pillow receiving one, two holy tears—holy with the having been there, holy with the dance we had seen a saint dance.

The chant began at 7 p.m. At first it was slow and subdued. Gurumayi sang, *Om Namo Bhagavate Muktanandaya,* her eyes shut, her robed body swaying gently from side to side. In the manner of the Siddha Yoga tradition, the hall full of devotees responded with the same words, an ocean of sound. Gradually Gurumayi began to pick up the pace, patting her knees to indicate that the musicians should do likewise. The energy in the hall intensified as the chant quickened, voices growing stronger with each repetition of the words, Gurumayi's body becoming steadily more animated.

I had never seen Gurumayi get out of her chair to chant until that night. It was as if she didn't rise of her own volition. It was as if the force of chanting her beloved guru's name unfolded her legs, lifted her up, pulled her onto her feet, and all of us—hundreds of us—onto ours. Even seventy-four-year-old Mary, usually so reserved, rocked side-to-side next to me, her arms over her head; even I, usually not at home in my overweight, middle-aged body, for once was rinsed clean of self-consciousness, for once experienced my body as a temple. For how could we hold tight to anything, watching Gurumayi? *Anything:* stiffness, fear, resistance of any kind.

She swayed, she rocked, sweat glazing her beautiful brown face, tears pooling in her black eyes, pouring from her like grace. I longed to wipe the sweat from her face. Her hair flew in and out of her eyes, her head flipping side to side, faster, faster, until I worried that the force of her joy would snap her neck. Baba Muktanandya's name fell and fell from her lips like flowers, her entire sweet beautiful body quivering with her devotion to him, the ecstasy in her muffled, unbounded. Gurumayi's devotees were chanting to honor her on the day of her birth, but she could think only of her own guru, the one who spent his long life polishing her so fine, so beautiful, in order that we might see ourselves reflected in her—that we might discover our own divinity in her ecstatic face.

She laughed and laughed. Like a jazz musician at the height of her powers, she played with the lines of the chant, often improvising. *Muktanandya, oh Muktanandya,* she chanted, over and over. Each time she waited for us to answer, and we did, our eyes riveted on her to see what would come next, our bodies in constant motion, the throng of us. Sometimes she would gesture to the lead singers and musicians to take the chant and run with it. They would improvise—singers, keyboard player, cellist, drummers—and Gurumayi would dance with abandon. Then, in a heartbeat, she would stop: silence, a stretched-out, potent silence. Her black eyes were on us, always that smile playing on her lips, her body still, as if storing up. Then she would spring, and the musicians—sprung—would start again, the drummers' hands hot on the skins of the drums, the heat of their palms not to be imagined.

Gurumayi had let fall away from her the sturdiness she usually shows us, the still, serene mountain of her that we are accustomed to. That night she let us see with our own eyes the bliss that is her constant state, the pure joy she swims in every moment she lives. Her letting go that way got into our veins, lifted us from the earth, took us to a place we had not been. Her visible ecstasy was an invitation to us to experience wholly our own divinity.

Hours and hours it went on, the intensity of the chant and the dance mounting. Sometimes a head in the crowd would turn, look to the side, eyes grabbing onto the eyes of someone nearby, as if to say, *Is this really happening?* We had never seen Gurumayi like this before. Some of us had spent time with her for many years, and she had never been like this.

Finally she was spent, her voice nearly gone. At 11 she began to slow us down. She grew quiet and still again herself. She sat back down in her chair, folding her legs beneath her silk robes the color of fire. Most of us were still on our feet, still revved, unable to feel earth under us again. Gurumayi talked us down gently, steadily, until at last we were all sitting again, our hearts returning to their accustomed speed, sweat drying on our faces, cooling.

After she had calmed us with her soft, slow voice, like a mother quieting her over-excited children, she said, *Some of you may be here for the first time. We don't usually get this way.* She laughed her deep laugh. Then she said, *It is time for you all to go home now. The fairies in your beds have been wondering where you've been: they've been asking, what is keeping them so long?* Tenderly, like a lullabye, her words soothed us, as if she were stroking our wet faces with her hand. *It is time to go to your beds and sleep. Tomorrow will come fast, dear ones. You must get up tomorrow and live your lives.*

She saw it in our faces, saw it plain in our eyes, in the tears that would not cease their spilling, that she had taken us the way a lover takes a beloved. Nothing would be the same after that. She might get us to leave her, she might move us toward our beds, but there would be no return to whatever our lives had been before that night.

At last I felt ready to stand, go back to the dorm, and sleep. Mary indicated that she was ready as well. We thought the night was over. I said to myself, Now Gurumayi will stand, look at us all one long last time, and then walk out of the hall. As always, I knew we would forget to breathe as we watched her walk up the aisle, turn, and move through the door. Then we would all stand, go back to our dorms, as she said we must, and try to sleep. We waited for her to stand.

To the surprise of everyone in the hall, Gurumayi began to speak again. Almost in a whisper, she said, *I am going to sit here until you all go.* It seemed she was saying we had to tear ourselves from her, that she would not leave the hall first. Then Gurumayi said—I could not make myself believe I was hearing her say these words—*I am going to sit here and you can come for darshan, and then you must go.*

For many months there had been no darshan line, no chance to come close to her to receive her blessing, to bow before her. I could hardly believe there would be more to this blessed night, that she had yet more to give. Mary and I sat still and watched the line form in front of Gurumayi, men and women and children standing ten abreast in their stocking feet, a stream of humanity in absolute, dumb struck love with her. All the while the musicians continued to play the music of the chant, slowly and very softly. The long line crept toward her, the movement almost imperceptible. We watched her lift a glass of water to her mouth, to soothe her throat that the words of the chant had tumbled over like jewels for so many hours. We watched her look at the faces moving toward her, the heads bowing at her feet. I drank it all in until I thought I would die of happiness. The knowledge that soon Mary and I would be moving toward her was a larger thing, almost, than my heart could contain.

At last Mary and I stood and moved to join the darshan line. The time spent inching toward Gurumayi's light was the sweetest waiting of my life. My stocking feet barely felt the carpeted floor beneath them. My mind was aware only fleetingly of the person in front of me, and the next one up, and the next, as far as I could see. Though I could not see her then, knowing I was coming closer and closer to Gurumayi made my heart a wild drum in my chest. It was only a matter of time before the last head in front of mine would sink to her feet, revealing her like the suddenly risen sun.

At last there was nothing and no one between us. She sat like Everest with her hands on her knees, her red silk robes around her like the fire of the sun. Her black hair was disheveled. She did not smile or speak. She let me into her black bottomless eyes, whose depth is not to be fathomed—those eyes that cannot look anyplace that they do not find God.

Gurumayi looked at my face, at the transparency of my loving her so hard. I thought my heart would crack. I sank to my knees and laid my heart at her feet like a tender animal. I touched my forehead to the rug at her feet and raised my face again. Inside I said, *Dearest Gurumayi, how can it be that I love you more than I did?* She could see nothing in my face but God. And for that timeless moment that I will hold on my tongue and taste over and over again until I die—for once in my life—I saw reflected in her eyes the thing that she saw.

JAN FRAZIER is a poet and writing teacher living in western Massachusetts. She has been practicing Siddha Yoga since 1990.

DONALD L. ROSE

Symbols among the Angels

THE TABERNACLE set up by ancient Israelites in the Sinai wilderness was an epitome of symbolism. Dorothea Harvey, in *The Holy Center* says that the tabernacle was the sign for Israel of God's intent to hold a continuing place in their midst. [1] Within the holy place there was a golden table and upon the table there was bread. The bread itself, says Swedenborg, was a symbol, standing for "that food by which it- self angels live." [2]

In Swedenborg's visits to the spiritual world, he learned that an- gels live by the satisfaction of accomplishing something of benefit to others. When they are able to bring their love into action, they are enlivened and rejuvenated.[3] Jesus himself said to the disciples, "My food is to do the will of him who sent me, and to finish his work."[4] Just as the Psalmist recalls that "man did eat angels' food",[5] we cher- ish our experience of harmonious action, and we are sustained when with our hands or talents we have made a difference.

"Heaven is a kingdom of uses," Swedenborg often said, and sym- bolically heaven is a great "house of bread" whose fragments nour- ish the inhabitants of earth. To see into this kingdom and to be with angels was the gift Swedenborg had in extraordinary measure. From his testimony we garner the following symbols.

Swedenborg reports seeing an angel wearing a symbolic badge. Within a circle of diamonds was pictured a golden eagle on the top of a tree, sheltering her young.[6] The eagle symbol evokes farsighted vision and elevated perspective, and the wings convey besides pro- tection the ability to be lifted up. Though our feet be planted on the ground, we can identify with the eagle in that we know the yearning to rise above the trivial and pedestrian preoccupations of life.

Marc Chagall.
Blue Angel. Gouache
and pastel, 20×26 in.
The Armand Hammer
Foundation, Los Angeles.

Once awakening from a dream, Swedenborg saw something obviously symbolic. "There seemed to descend from heaven a long roll fastened to rods, and tied by most beautiful woven knots of an azure color; the beauty of this object was indescribable. It was said that the angels make such presents to one another."[7] So angels give presents to one another! Think about it. What do you give to the person who has everything? Angels have all they need.[8] We give something with meaning. Angels might give a beautiful scroll, or some other symbol.

And what would angels give to an old gentleman near the end of his days? Inside the cover of one of Swedenborg's books is a list of gifts, "valuables" received from angels.

He had previously mentioned symbolic gifts he received, a pomegranate with seeds of gold, a cluster of grapes whose leaves became silver, fragrant twigs tipped with gold. They were mementos of visits to angel communities.[9] The final list of gifts includes things we can visualize:

- A beautiful red chest, consisting of five rows,
  five drawers in each row.

- A beautiful little rose containing a brilliant diamond

- A box in a casket wherein are shining crystals, signifying rebirth to eternity.

But at the end of the list the imagery eludes us, for he only says, "something precious which cannot be seen by spirits but only by angels."[10]

And so we stop to consider that the people of ancient Israel saw bread to be a symbol of something heavenly. Jesus related bread to the fulfillment we feel in accomplishing work. Swedenborg spoke of heaven as a kingdom of uses. It was his belief that the realm of nature was full of symbols of that heavenly kingdom. He wrote "There is nothing beautiful and delightful in the skies or on the earth which is not in some way representative of (that) kingdom."[11] Finally he felt privileged to explore in spirit the heavenly realms, and there he saw gifts that were beautiful and filled with enduring meaning.

DONALD L. ROSE has worked as a pastor in Europe, Australia, and the United States. He now edits *New Church Life*, a magazine devoted to the insights revealed through Emanuel Swedenborg.

Notes

1. Dorothea Harvey. *The Holy Center: A Biblical Path to the Presence Within.* New York: Swedenborg Foundation, 1983.

2. Emanuel Swedenborg. *Arcana Coelestia.* West Chester, Pennsylvania: Swedenborg Foundation, 1998. First published in Latin, 8 volumes, 1749–1756. Paragraph 3478.

3. *Ibid.,* Paragraph 5147:3

4. John 4.

5. Psalm 78, verse 24.

6. Swedenborg. *Marital Love.* West Chester, Pennsylvania: Swedenborg Publishing Association Foundation, 1975. Paragraph 15.

7. Swedenborg. *Arcana.* Paragraph 6492.

8. Swedenborg. *Heaven and Hell.* West Chester, Pennsylvania: Swedenborg Foundation, 1995. Paragraph 190.

9. Swedenborg. *Marital Love.* Paragraphs 75–77.

10. Cyriel Odhner Sigstedt. *The Swedenborg Epic.* London: Swedenborg Society, 1981, pp. 422, 480.

11. Swedenborg. *Arcana.* Paragraph 1807.

CATHERINE LAZERS BAUER

In Praise of Trees

Did you know trees talk? Well they do. They talk to each other, and they'll talk to you if you listen. Trouble is, white people don't listen.
—TATANGA MANI, STONEY INDIAN
TOUCH THE EARTH, D. T. C. MCLUHAN

IN PLANTING TWO BOX ELDERS in the side yard the day I was born, perhaps my grandfather also implanted my love for trees. Members of the solid and respectable maple family, box elders are nevertheless considered poor relations—soft skeletons in a hardwood closet, the dandelions of the tree world. Box elders grow easily and well; they never learned to play hard to get. But maybe a Depression baby rated Depression trees.

Did you ever see a box elder for sale in a nursery? Blue spruce, mountain ash, Russian olive, Norway maple; but box elder? Even the afterlife of this lowly tree is unimpressive. Whoever heard of a box elder armoire or solid box elder paneling in a drawing room? But, my birthday trees were like the lovable mongrel that wags its tail, follows a kid home from school, and becomes the faithful, favored family pet. The box elders set a worthy example. Simple, honest, sturdy, and unpretentious, they grew into fine shade trees that didn't need to put on airs. They just put on leaves. Like a deft puppeteer, the biggest box elder maneuvered my motions at the end of a rope that held a tire. From heavy chains slung around their waists, the trees held my hammock.

*Catherine
Lazers Bauer*

AFTER I GREW UP, a big black walnut tree grew near my country garden. "They're becoming scarce," my neighbor said. "Why don't you sell it? It shades your garden." Then the clincher, "It would bring a right good price." But I make friends with trees. How often I'd wished I could press my ear to its trunk and listen to its secrets about our antecedents who chopped the same black earth and gathered corn and tomatoes from the garden plot. You'd no more *sell* a friend than you'd neglect one in time of need.

When our locust tree in Ohio was desperately in need, we moved swiftly, taking an ailing branch to the county agent. He prescribed an antidote. It was an evening in late June while I was working in the vegetable garden that Ralph got out the chemicals and spray equipment and proceeded to treat our locust. He sprayed it top to bottom, saturating the leaves, before discovering he'd used weed killer instead of the antidote.

Then he walked toward my garden where I was weeding squash and beans. The last streak of pink was slipping behind the world

when I heard my name being called ever so softly. I saw Ralph's shadowy outline in the dusk. "Katy, come here and tell me you love me," he said.

With hoses, we soaked and doused and flooded that tree until it wept waterfalls by starlight. Nevertheless, the leaves browned and fell lifeless to the ground. We had high hopes that it would come back the following spring, but only the topmost branches gave any hint of life. The effect was bizarre—a skeleton wearing a feathery tufted toupee of yellow green.

Ralph took as a personal affront the few allusions I made to the sad tree, so we both sort of looked the other way when we were near it. But in midsummer, snippets of green popped out on lower branches, and by September, our full-leafed locust laughed and called it spring.

Eventually, the tree forgave us our trespass and got back on schedule, budding in springtime, dropping leaves in autumn. A patient silence had been our only recourse. When you wish so much to relieve a hurt or mend a quarrel . . . occasionally, it just takes time. When you want to say the most, you ache inside and say the least.

NOW WE LIVE IN THE COLORADO FOOTHILLS, a land of scenic wonder compared to the gray industrial flatlands of Ohio. Depending on the season, Turkey Creek rushes or trickles past our door. Doubleheader Mountain monitors our days.
Everywhere are Ponderosa pines. Beautiful, tall, proud pines. Twisted, skinny, scraggly pines. They fill our six acres to the north, south, east, and when we came, to the west. Our good neighbor, a forester, reminded us soon after we arrived that there were many beetle-infested trees on the south slope west of the house. "They'll have to come down," he said. "The beetles start flying in late July."

He marked the trees, tying scarlet plastic ribbons in their hair. From the house I heard the roar of the chain saw, the loud cracking of splitting wood, the crashing thud of tall trees hitting the ground. Three days it took to fell 33 trees that took 80 years and more to inch their way toward the Colorado sky.
My husband, our neighbor, a lad we hired, and I pitched into the task of stacking piles of cut wood. The gray cross sections got sprayed with insecticide. The battlefield became thick with felled trunks and severed limbs.

There's something sacrilegious about replacing a forest with black-plastic-shrouded mounds. One is tempted to place

Trees. Jon Luoma.
Silk-screen print, 1975.

a wreath of the prolific Rocky Mountain wildflowers (Columbine, Penstemon, Cutleaf Daisy, and Indian Paintbrush) atop the brittle burial mounds, except that, too, would be a kind of added desecration.

Some say it's nature's way. Only man wants trees to live forever. There is, after all, a ruthless unconcern for the scheme of things. There is also universal calm and order. Rather than contemplate, I chose to fill my wheelbarrow with small young pines that grew in our septic system's leach bed. "They'll need transplanting," the former owner had said, pointing to the thick new growth, "or the roots will cause trouble."

I hauled the saplings to the barren slope along with gallon jugs of water. The hose would never reach that far. I wheeled my barrow across a narrow footbridge, but couldn't push it up the steep slope on the other side. Back and forth I went, emptying my vehicle of its contents, slinging young pines and a spade over my shoulder, carrying jugs of water in my free hand, then reloading my vehicle. I laughed aloud comparing myself to pioneers who'd met mountains and emptied their Conestoga wagons so the beasts could haul them up sharp inclines.

That's not all I laughed at. I remembered how smug we were. "No yard work!" we boasted to incredulous friends in Ohio. "In the mountains the terrain is as is . . . trees, wildflowers, rock outcroppings, and natural ground cover. *No grass cutting!*"

"None at all?" There was envy in our neighbor's eyes.

"Nosiree! Not in the mountains," Ralph echoed. And to a hallelujah chorus, we sold our lawnmowers.

But in the mountains of Colorado, my husband has been sleeping with a heating pad tucked beneath his back and pillows stuffed under his knees.

Lying in the dark stillness of the night, I heard Ralph groan as he shifted position. "Your Majesty," he said to no one in particular, "these peons have no grass to cut."

Then in a falsetto, he paraphrased the insensitive Marie Antoinette. "Aha! Then let them cut trees!" I smiled, but only a little. As Bernard Malamud reminds, "Suffering also makes for laughter."

CATHERINE LAZERS BAUER has sold more than 550 essays, articles, and stories to national, regional, and literary markets, including *The Christian Science Monitor, Spiritual Life, American Poet Quarterly,* and *Bloomsbury Review.*

JOHN L. HITCHCOCK

Jimmy Christ

SOMETIMES, AS I WASH JIMMY'S body, it assumes the awkward form that Mexican artists mastered in their carvings of crucifixions or pietas, and I feel that I am preparing the Christ for burial and not Jimmy for his day's work at the care center. Or am I preparing the Christ in Jimmy for another day of teaching and bringing love?

Nancy Hartley had a normal pregnancy, joyfully expectant of her first child. That was forty years ago. In the birth, however, all changed. The baby turned, and the umbilical twisted around its neck, so that the birth became a hanging. But Jimmy lived, and the Hartleys were also changed, all their hopes rewritten. The continuous crucifixion—suspension on the cross of radical need—had come.

I believe that such visitations are for our sakes. Out of birth, death; out of death, life.

Alan Magee.
Starometské.
Acrylic on board,
10×15 in, 1989.

Jimmy has no words. With labored movements, he can swing his arm over to indicate the "yes" or "no" signs on the arms of his wheelchair, but if I am to really discover his needs, I must use my creativity to guess and ask him if that's what it is. I try to catch the quick nod or shake and save Jimmy the labor of his muscles and concentration, but with him that's not an issue. He wants the exchange, whatever it takes.

I have always felt that I needed to *pay* for my place in the world by *doing*. But now like the Christ, Jimmy gives to all in *being* served. I am forced to honor being, and I don't really know how. I know that there are those who give more than enough just in being objects of care.

The boy–man is beautiful. Eternal youth at forty years. We say that his body failed to develop, but is that the essence of the thing? What has developed instead?

Jimmy lives to cooperate; this is his freedom. His freedom might have been to rebel, and if I am to claim freedom, the choice is the same: to assert myself in defiance, or to assert myself in love. Jimmy is happy. He has created a loving space in the unforseen demands of the Hartleys' lives.

As I feed Jimmy each spoonful of his breakfast, I touch the side of his head to remind him where it is. One of the effects of cerebral palsy is the loss of awareness of where such things as arms, legs, and heads are at the moment. The longer he can keep his head up, the better chance he has of swallowing. Often, his eyes suddenly turn to me, and we smile at each other. Sometimes, he just rests the side of his head against my hand. Those moments are profound, though I can't say why. I'm so used to thinking, but this wordless communion is a new way for me.

I often wonder what the Hartleys' life would be like if Jimmy were now, say, on his way up somewhere in business. Would they be as devoted and loving as they are now? Do they regret their confinement? I don't believe so. Jimmy centers their lives; his helplessness draws them out of themselves. We'd all benefit from such a concrete Christ.

I grew up with an old hymn about the Christ waiting outside the door and knocking. It haunted me; to a child, it sounded like such a simple thing to do to open the door. But where was that door? I wanted to be told what to do in so many words. Whatever it is that wants entrance is rather helpless after all, and certainly is unable to use words.

When my work is done, I leave; and the fact that Jimmy and his parents are in this together all day, every day, goes with me. But that's how it is; if we can leave the suffering, we will. We avoid pain at all costs, yet something nags at me from within, telling me that I also am "in it," that I am being called by a suffering, helpless figure, wounded not by an accident at birth, but by neglect in my life, its brain partially killed for lack of blood.

We think of the Christ as king—power, dominion, and glory—but he is also the Child of the Christmas story, the new birth within our humanity, *born* to rule, to be sure, but undiscovered, except by the Wise. In each of us the Christ is helpless, must be washed, diapered, fed, and loved.

Am I exploiting Jimmy's innocence with these thoughts? No, that feeling comes from what I fail to do about the call, from within, of the Anointed One whom I can't hear and see nearly as well as I do this person whom I am paid to help.

And it also is right that we don't deliberately seek out suffering. However, *when* it comes, as it *does*, suffering is the calling card of the Christ, the knock on the door. It calls us to compassion, but not only, or even primarily, for the suffering of others in the usual sense.

If we had real compassion toward ourselves, we would stop hiding from the pain in our own lives. If our inner lives were as straitened as the lives of the Hartleys, we would find the way to wisdom. What holds them to the path is that a helpless carrier of love needs nurturing, and without blaming themselves they see the *givenness* of the event that came to them forty years ago.

All of the hurts that we have patched over without really doing the work of healing; all the wounds that we have hidden behind a facade of competence; all of our pride in "just going on;" all our failures to seek forgiveness; these are what gradually blind us to the suffering of the life of love lost within. But to be aware of such facts requires our openness to something as concrete to us as Jimmy is to the Hartleys, if only we could see ourselves with depth and clarity.

It's not terribly dramatic—the continuous crucifixion—this daily caring for the fragile and wounded—although by no means is it devoid of joy. The Hartleys celebrate every day. Perhaps it's the sense of having a purpose; perhaps it's staying with the indicated course of love; perhaps it's the honoring of innocence. I'm grateful for Jimmy's presence, emblematic of a sacred path.

JOHN HITCHCOCK is a family therapist in northeast Iowa. He has taught mythology as well as astronomy at San Francisco State University, and physics at the University of Wisconsin at La Crosse. Since 1968 Dr. Hitchcock has led seminars with the Guild for Psychological Studies of San Francisco, specializing in mythology and in science as a source of numinous symbols for personal growth.

DON KISSIL

Flying

THE FLOWERS IN TOWN ON THAT WARM MAY MORNING were as bright and cheerful as they would be all year. The snows had begun to melt in the Austrian Alps surrounding Innsbruck, but the tourists had not yet arrived en masse. Claire and I decided to see what spring flowers and birds had arrived at the top of the Nordkette cable-car lift. In that radiant morning sun, we walked without a care along the Inns River to the funicular that would take us some 7,600 feet up the mountain peak. After boarding, we slowly swung our way to the first stop.

On that particular morning all the funicular cars were empty, save for us and another, younger, couple. Anticipating language difficulties, I hesitated to engage them in conversation. Their faces were solemn and they talked only a little.

At the first stop I finally heard the woman speak. Her German was peppered with a strong central European accent. He spoke in monosyllables in a Tyrolian dialect which even the best German speakers cannot completely comprehend. If they knew we were there, their guarded tones clearly suggested they had chosen to not recognize our presence. Claire and I nattered about the snow and the flowers, but also in hushed voices. As the door slammed shut, we rocked and shook towards our next and final step.

On this leg the mist settled around us, and the wet snow on the ground appeared quite dense. The car temperature had dropped noticeably. The ride was only seven or eight minutes long, but we rose at such a steep angle that I began to gulp and swallow air, as one does in an elevator that shoots too swiftly upward. Still there was no contact between us and the young couple.

We bumped into the last station. As the doors slid open the man immediately jumped out and seemed to vanish. The woman stepped out onto the landing and we followed. Claire and I zipped our ski jackets and searched our pockets for gloves.

Sir Anthony van Dyck. *Daedalus and Icarus.* Oil on canvas, 115.3×86.4 cm., ca. 1620. Art Gallery of Ontario, Toronto, Gift of Mr. and Mrs. Frank P. Wood, 1940.

As strangers often do in new situations, I relied on the weather to break the ice. "Damn cold up here, and some difference from down below." She looked at me with piercing dark eyes but a gentle smile and said: "Oh, you're English."

"No, American. And you?"

"I'm Rumanian, from Kishinev. Do you know where that is? Few Americans know anything about Rumania except for our famous Transylvanian Dracula."

"Kishinev, eh? That's in Moldavia," I replied, a bit smug in knowing I had shattered her image of the geographically challenged American. I also told her that my mother was born in Kishinev, so perhaps I had cheated a bit.

Her dark eyes brightened as she nodded her acknowledgment, and I immediately began to sense the "landsmann" develop. That's the European equivalent of our "homeboy" thing. So I followed quickly with: "Where has your *mann* disappeared?"

I had used the German word for husband. She quickly corrected me by replying that Bertil was only her boyfriend, not her husband. She said that he would appear in a moment or so, which he did, in a big way.

A momentary clearing of the mist exposed Bertil atop the cable car with a huge nylon bag balanced precariously on his shoulder. It was nearly twenty feet long. He had one arm crooked under and around it and his other extended to steady it, as he jumped onto the landing alongside the car. With the bag still balanced on his shoulder, he ran through the slushy snow past us toward an open field near the edge of the mountain.

"What *is* that thing he's carrying?" Claire asked.

"It's probably a big kite." I whispered.

Bertil laid the bag on the ground and unzipped it along its length, exposing an enormous, brilliant red and yellow butterfly which he quickly removed from its cocoon, spreading its wings.

"A hang glider," I exploded. The thin air carried my voice to him and for the first time he looked directly at me. As we made eye contact he smiled, a small but unfulfilled smile that made my stomach a bit queasy.

I quickly turned away and asked his girlfriend the inappropriate question: "Here, in the Alps, in this weather, is he mad? Why does he do this?"

"If you are truly descended from Rumanian stock," she challenged us softly, "you would probably be interested in a good story. If you and your lady would be so kind as to join me for a coffee while Bertil suits up and checks his winds, I will tell you the tale."

The woman was tall and thin and, despite her heavy boots, had the tiny feet of a ballerina. She carried her backpack like an athlete as she led us to a small table surrounded by four benches near the back of the car barn. She moved with an air of someone who had been here many times before.

The woman, whose name I still did not know, pulled a large thermos filled with hot coffee from her backpack along with some plastic cups, and placed them carefully on the table before us. Reaching into her pack again, she produced a small bottle of schnapps and poured a hefty kiss into her empty cup. She held up the bottle, silently asking if we would like the same. Equally without words, both Claire and I nodded, *yes.*

She removed her cap and tossed it onto a nail near the window. Her long, shiny, black hair stayed tied in a schoolteacher's bun. We relaxed into the steaming hot coffee and the sound of her voice as she began her story.

"Bertil is the son of a Tyrolian civil servant, a postman in fact. And Franz, Bertil's father, as a young man, was extremely well-read in Greek mythology. Franz dreamed of flying like Icarus to the sun. Many years before the hang gliding craze had taken hold, Franz had been inventing and reinventing different types of lifting kites, gliding and soaring devices. As a true Tyrol, Franz also loved his mountains where it was quiet and not only could his imagination soar but someday, with his inventions, his body would as well.

"Franz married young, and to his very opposite type. She was a hot-blooded Spaniard from Andalusia, Seville, I believe, who was as grounded and earthy as Franz was airborne. Lust and lovemaking was for Maritza as natural as eating and dancing. Maritza simply loved men. She loved to tease and tantalize them, and Franz tolerated her passions. Franz did this purely for his love of Maritza, as only those who truly love can understand.

"She was careful always to keep Franz happy and indulge his every whim. And thus, Maritza could maintain her double life—having numerous affairs—while Franz was off at work, delivering the mail."

I looked over at Claire to see how these very personal things the woman was saying were playing on her, but Claire's eyes were riveted on the storyteller. The lilt and timbre of her voice was hypnotic.

"Not long after their marriage Maritza became pregnant and Bertil was born. Still with the postal service, Franz relocated here, to Innsbruck, with Maritza and their young son. Maritza took to Innsbruck well enough, and as soon as possible, placed young Bertil in school, thus providing for her continued freedom. She took a part-time job as a waitress in a Spanish restaurant in the Alt Stadt. Franz built a workshop behind their rented house and spent much of his spare time working with his dreams and, in the evenings, taking care of young Bertil. Bertil came to love his father, and son and father bonded into each others' fantasies. But as the genes often determine, Bertil grew to have the fire of his mother and the soul of his father, and I can verify the truth of that.

"Bertil would often accompany his father up into the mountains to test one of Franz's new inventions. He learned the feeling for flight very early. He was light, strong, and fearless in the air, and Franz capitalized on his son's eagerness. Their trips into the mountains were a boon to Maritza. She could thus continue with the intrigues and affairs she loved, while they could indulge themselves in their work, unbothered by the need to return home at a prescribed time.

"As time progressed, Franz and Bertil built a small cabin right here on the mountain top, about a hundred meters up from where we now sit. They slowly transported all of Franz's workshop into it. As Bertil grew into his early twenties, he began to slowly break away from Franz, as, I believe, most young men will."

She took another sip of her schnapps-laced coffee and I said in the brief pause, "My dear young woman, I still do not know your name." Either she did not hear, or chose not to answer, for she simply picked up the thread of her story and continued.

I cannot deny that I was entranced by her tale.

She told things too private for strangers to hear. Many of them I cannot, or perhaps choose not, to remember. She studied linguistics while Bertil studied dentistry at the same university, the University of Bucharest in Rumania where they met. He was her first lover. During vacations she would accompany Bertil back to Innsbruck and there she met Maritza and Franz. She instantly liked his father— it was clear Bertil took after him—but Maritza frightened her. She could never quite understand why.

She and Bertil lived together for six years but never married. She taught languages at a local college in Rumania, but he never practiced his dentistry. He returned to Innsbruck to work as a ski instructor. She said she never married, but told of several lovers she'd taken over the course of the next five years. Imperceptible at first, her voice seemed to change, taking on an unexpected stridency.

"Then one evening I got this strange phone call from Bertil requesting that I come to Innsbruck immediately. No explanations, 'Just come,' he pleaded in a tone I had never heard him use before.

"It was about this time of year, in May, the evening we met at the train station in Innsbruck. I could immediately see that a great tragedy had somehow befallen him. From the station we quickly walked to that little upstairs restaurant in the old town, they call it the *Jörgele*. Perhaps you know it?"

She blew a light breath over the top of her coffee cup before taking another sip. I nodded and said we'd eaten there often. She continued.

"He did not speak, but, just as we reached the door of the steps leading up to the restaurant, Bertil grabbed me tightly, swung me around into his arms and kissed me hard on the lips. Not a passionate kiss, just a hard one and clearly full of anger. Then he said: 'Marry me!'

"His words did not reach me as quickly as the anger in his kiss, and I asked him what was the matter."

" 'Maritza is dead! Franz is lost, our cabin in the mountains is burned beyond repair, and I don't know what to do.' "

"We did not go into the restaurant, but moved off to a darkened bench in a nearby park where he buried his head in my arms and cried like a child.

"Get hold of yourself Bertil, and tell me what has happened. Shall we go for a drink? Please, speak to me!

"In a moment or two, he began to compose himself. He then told me what had happened quickly, almost spitting out the words as though he'd just eaten something foul!"

" 'You knew Maritza and her ways, as well as I did. Franz knew, all our friends did too, that mother liked to have many men in her life. But we never spoke of it. One day Franz went up to our mountain cabin and found her in his bed with one of the cable-car mechanics. He was a friend . . . my father and I had known him for years.

" 'Something must have snapped in Franz. The coroner said that Maritza was found wrapped in the arms of her lover and both were shot through the head at close range.

" 'The police told me that Franz tried to set fire to the cabin, but only his workshop area had burned. That small part in the back of the workshop where Franz and I would sometimes sleep, that had not burned. And that's where they found the two of them.

" 'They found my father's flying harness at the edge of the mountainside at our favorite jumping off place, but did not find his wings.

" 'It is the judgment of the police that Franz killed them both and jumped off the mountainside with only his wings, to try and fly away. His body has not yet been found and it's been more than two weeks.

" 'Somehow, damn it, I feel he is not buried in the snow as the police insist, but still up there, flying about. I'm devastated and lost. I don't know what to do. I must try to find Franz.

" 'When I was a boy he would tell me the story of Icarus and how, when he angered the gods, they killed him. But if I was a good boy, the gods would never kill me—and someday I, too, would fly with wings of my own. I soon came to know the difference between his dreams and reality but I'm not so certain that Franz ever did.

" 'My dear friend,' he said, with a wistfulness in his voice that I could remember from when we were still lovers, "Help me to find Franz. Help me to find my father. For I know in my heart he's flying around out there, waiting for me.'"

"Without thinking, I said, 'But what can I do?'"

"'Come with me up to the top of Nordkette Lift and help me search. Tomorrow morning, at first light, we will go by funicular and with your help I will suit up in my own wings to search the thermals for Franz.'"

"And I did just that, then. And today as well. Just as I have done every year on this same day for the past five years. Bertil soars and kettles down and about the mountains searching for his father, and, somehow, I support his search.

"No, we never married. I still teach at the same college in Rumania, and he still gives ski lessons, but we meet here each year to continue the search. Oh, yes, I know it's futile. But how else can I be with my lover and my friend who has never lost his dream to fly?

"Care for another schnapps? Bertil will be ready at any moment now and I must take him his coffee and give him a kiss goodbye before he jumps.

"OH, YES MY NAME IS ALSO MARITZA," she winked, flashing a saucy smile, "but I'm nothing like Bertil's mother. Tschüss!"

DON KISSIL was borne more than sixty years ago in the Bronx, New York, but now lives in New Jersey. A licensed pharmacist by academic training, he has worked as a research scientist, medical writer, advertising copywriter, and, for almost thirty years, as a freelance writer. He has written and published much nonfiction and now writes fiction for children. He has written a novel on the Maya, several picture books dealing with Mayan myths, and many short stories.